The RDA

D0354935

A Guide for the Occasional Cataloger

Amy Hart

 LINWORTH

AN IMPRINT OF ABC-CLIO, LLC
Santa Barbara, California • Denver, Colorado • Oxford, England

Copyright 2010 by ABC-CLIO, LLC

Library of Congress Cataloging-in-Publication Data

Hart, Amy.
  The RDA primer : a guide for the occasional cataloger / Amy Hart.
      p. cm.
  Includes bibliographical references and index.
  ISBN 978-1-58683-348-0 (acid-free paper) — ISBN 978-1-59884-747-5 (ebook)   1. Resource description & access.   2. Descriptive cataloging—Standards.   I. Title.
  Z694.15.R47H37   2010
  025.3'2—dc22   2010022964

ISBN: 978-1-58683-348-0
EISBN: 978-1-59884-747-5

14   13   12   11   10   1   2   3   4   5

This book is also available on the World Wide Web as an eBook.
Visit www.abc-clio.com for details.

Linworth
An Imprint of ABC-CLIO, LLC

ABC-CLIO, LLC
130 Cremona Drive, P.O. Box 1911
Santa Barbara, California 93116-1911

This book is printed on acid-free paper (∞)

Manufactured in the United States of America

Contents

Figures

About the Author

Amy Hart entered the library profession as AACR2 was being implemented. She always wondered what it would be like to live through implementation of a revised cataloging code and is now finding out. Amy earned her Diploma in Library and Information Studies at the University College Dublin, Ireland. She has worked in special, school, public, and academic libraries. She is currently director of technical services for the Minuteman Library Network in Massachusetts.

Introduction

Who Is This Book For?

This book introduces the new cataloging code, Resource Description and Access (RDA), to librarians who need a general understanding of how it works and the basics of how to use it. Librarians who do some cataloging, in addition to all their other duties, should find it useful. The intended audience may include School Librarians, Special Librarians, one-person library Librarians, as well as Copy Catalogers, Paraprofessional staff, and Library and Information Science students.

Explaining RDA is complicated by its dual purposes. While it seeks to simplify cataloging rules, it also seeks to transform cataloging, bringing it in-line with 21st-century Web technologies. Nonetheless, at a basic level, RDA remains a content standard for library cataloging; it delineates rules for what is included in a catalog entry and how the information should be recorded. This, in turn, affects anyone working in a library—anyone whose position includes describing library resources, providing access to resources, or helping patrons to discover resources—in other words, *you*.

Cataloging is sometimes viewed as separate from the public side of library work. But it should be considered an integral part of user services. To provide good service, a two-way discussion about what kinds of data are and need to be recorded about resources is essential. In addition, the future of cataloging is in a state of flux. RDA's goals, particularly regarding metadata, offer an opportunity for all librarians to influence how cataloging changes, who will do it, and how it is done. If you want a seat at the table, RDA offers you the opportunity.

How Is This Book Organized?

The book is organized to trace the development of RDA, starting with the why, and who, and how, and moving onward until we reach the content, format, and implications for you.

- Chapter 1 discusses the history and development of RDA, beginning with why the new rules were warranted and how AACR2 (*Anglo-American Cataloging Rules, Revised*) became RDA.

- Chapter 2 looks at the conceptual models that form the backbone for RDA—FRBR (Functional Requirements for Bibliographic Data) and FRAD (Functional Requirements for Authority Data). Without an understanding of FRBR and FRAD, RDA cannot make much sense.

- Chapter 3 continues the discussion of FRBR and FRAD with a look at the entities identified in them. The FRBR and FRAD conceptual models are built on entity-relationship analysis. As such, their major components are entities and their attributes and the relationships possible between entities. This chapter looks at entities and attributes.

- Chapter 4 concludes our review of FRBR and FRAD with a discussion of the kinds of relationships that each identify as existing between entities.

- Chapter 5 turns from RDA's foundations to RDA itself. It looks at RDA through the prism of AACR2, comparing the structures of the two cataloging standards. It will be most useful to those familiar with AACR2. The chapter also looks at some of the FRBR-based vocabulary of RDA.

- Chapter 6 reviews how RDA differs from AACR2, starting with its bedrock principles and moving on to specific rule changes.

- Chapter 7 looks at the changes that have been made to the MARC format in order to accommodate the implementation of RDA.

- Chapter 8 takes what we learned in chapters 5–7 and applies it to the cataloging process. It walks through the steps of descriptive cataloging using RDA, noting where rules may be located and where practice has changed.

- Chapter 9 starts in the present and moves toward the future. It looks at the impact of RDA on integrated library systems (ILS) and asks what changes are needed for its short-term implementation. The chapter then moves into the future and wonders what kinds of changes might lie ahead if libraries wish to fulfill RDA's promise of being cataloging rules for the 21st century.

- Chapter 10 introduces the work of the DCMI/RDA Task Group. The Dublin Core Metadata Initiative (DCMI) worked with the developers of RDA to ensure that RDA would be a viable metadata standard. Specifically, this chapter looks at the Semantic Web tools that the Task Group used to meet this goal.

- Chapter 11 looks more closely at the specific goals of the DCMI/RDA Task Group and how they were met. It looks at the RDA Element Sets and Vocabularies being registered at the National Science Digital Library (NSDL) Registry. It ends with a look at a similar initiative by the Library of Congress to make the Library of Congress Subject Headings available to the metadata community.

- Chapter 12 concludes the book with a look at how RDA will likely affect you in your library. It attempts to summarize what was covered and bring it down to earth. How will the immediate introduction of RDA affect library catalogs and resource discovery? What might the future hold?

A Special Note

This book is based on the November 2008 full draft of RDA that was released to the public in PDF format. It was written prior to the June 2010 publication of the online *RDA Toolkit* and the summer 2010 release of RDA in print. RDA's implementation is an ongoing process with decisions on how some parts of RDA will translate into cataloging practice yet to be made. In writing this book it was not always possible to know exactly how a rule will be applied.

How to Use This Book

My overall aim in writing this book was to be thorough and informative but in as light-handed a way as possible. While the book should flow nicely if read front to back, it is also possible to cut into specific chapters if you have a particular question or interest. Hence, the chapters on FRBR stand on their own, providing a basic understanding of the topic. Likewise, if you are only interested in the major changes between AACR2 and RDA, chapter 6 fits the bill. My goal was to provide practical information in small enough chunks so that you can easily absorb it and apply it to your own situation.

CHAPTER 1

History and Development of RDA

This chapter reviews the key organizations and committees that participated in RDA's development and lays out the governance of cataloging rules in general. It addresses the need to revise AACR2, including the need to internationalize cataloging standards, to broaden their applicability to electronic resources, and to devise structures that lend themselves to technological developments in the manipulation of information. It discusses the process that moved from AACR3 to RDA to a FRBR-ized structure, and the implications of the Library of Congress's (LC's) Working Group Report.

Machiavellian Intrigue

Describing the development of RDA is complicated because of the many dips, turns, and reversals along the way. Of course, these were to be expected in a process involving librarians (catalogers, no less). But in a bigger sense, there were bound to be problems from the start because of the goals set out. It is a tricky proposition to merely revise something at the same time that you are transforming it.

For many librarians, the goal of RDA was a straightforward update of cataloging rules. They hoped the revised rules would provide sensible guidelines for newer formats and address other ongoing issues with the code. They were not looking to upset the apple cart or to define completely new ways to do things.

For others, RDA was an opportunity, a last hope almost, to save the practice of cataloging from an increasingly fast plunge into an icy river. These librarians recognized that many nonlibrary constituencies were involving themselves in resource management and were reinventing our wheel with a more Web- and user-friendly approach. If catalogers are information managers extraordinaire (we've been doing this for centuries), shouldn't we have a seat at this table? Hence, an additional goal of RDA was to broaden its appeal to other kinds of organizations and to become compatible with metadata and Web technologies. To achieve these goals, RDA would need to transform cataloging.

For others still, RDA was a boondoggle, a project gone deeply wrong and unlikely to meet anybody's needs. With drafts running at lengths of over a thousand pages and language that confused more than clarified, many in the library community doubted the project could succeed. Even the LC, a member of the committee developing RDA, suggested at one point that work on it should stop.

As a result, things got complicated. But let's begin at the beginning.

Who Writes Cataloging Rules Anyway?

Since 1974 the Joint Steering Committee for Revision of AACR (JSC) has been responsible for the *Anglo-American Cataloging Rules*. In 2004 it began work on AACR3 (now titled RDA). The group is comprised of representatives from:

- American Library Association
- Library of Congress
- British Library
- Chartered Institute of Library and Information Professionals (CILIP) (UK)
- Canadian Committee on Cataloguing
- Australian Committee on Cataloguing

The JSC reports to the Committee of Principals (CoP), which oversees all work regarding the *Anglo-American Cataloging Rules,* including revisions, new editions, and publication. Members represent four of the JSC members (ALA, LC, the British Library, and CILIP) as well as the Canadian Library Association (CLA), Library and Archives Canada, and the National Library of Australia. Copyright of the *Rules* rests in the three national associations of the United States, Great Britain, and Canada—ALA, CILIP, and CLA ("AACR Governance").

As work progresses, drafts of the new cataloging code are made available to the interested communities. Various committees and organizations are charged with reviewing and submitting comments. The JSC takes these comments and revises accordingly.

Why Did We Need New Rules?

AACR2 came out in 1978 at a time when catalogs were housed in lovely, solid wood cabinets, records were printed on 3 × 5 cards and then filed, and most libraries had largely print collections. Since then, those cabinets have gone on the Internet to be sold and reused as CD cabinets, the cards have been thrown out or stockpiled as scrap paper, and our mostly print collections have been infiltrated by videos, DVDs, music CDs, audiobooks, downloadable audiobooks, electronic books, and, most recently, digital collections. Although the cataloging world and the JSC strove valiantly to revise AACR2 in response to the onslaught, the rules became increasingly creaky, unwieldy, and inappropriate.

The JSC's first draft of AACR3, part 1, cited these goals for the rules:

> The new edition of AACR is envisioned as providing the basis for improved user access to all media in an online search environment. It is being designed with a view to compatibility with other standards for resource description and retrieval and for use worldwide both by libraries and by other information agencies. The intent is to produce a new edition that will be easier and more efficient for cataloguers to use and interpret, both in a printed format and in an enhanced electronic form. ("Draft of AACR3")

Translated and expanded this means:

- Improved user access to all media in an online search environment
    - Make better rules for the new formats and media
    - Leverage power of online catalogs and the Web, don't just present a card catalog online
- Compatibility with other standards for resource description and retrieval

- Make library data discoverable and usable on the Web, both in- and outside of the library catalog
- For use worldwide both by libraries and by other information agencies
  - Make cataloging rules international rather than Anglo American in scope. Many non-English speaking countries have adopted AACR2 (translated to 25 languages, used in 45 countries; Glennan 1)
  - Publish cataloging rules as a metadata standard so that other kinds of organizations might be able to use it (museums, archives, publishers)
- Easier and more efficient for catalogers to use and interpret
  - Address problems in current rules:
    - Too many inconsistencies in rules
    - Not enough examples for nonprint formats
    - Rules are based on specific cases rather than on general principles
- An enhanced electronic format in addition to print
  - Recognize the power of Web-based, interactive interfaces for presenting information and make RDA available in this way

AACR3 to RDA

In April 2005, in response to community review of the draft, the JSC adjusted the scope and format of AACR3 and changed its name to RDA: Resource Description and Access ("Outcomes" 2005). Moving forward, the JSC would work toward:

- A more explicit connection to the Functional Requirements for Bibliographic Records (FRBR) and Functional Requirements for Authority Data (FRAD)
- A broader focus and more explicit connection to the metadata community
- Enough change to merit new rules, but backward compatibility with AACR2, to avoid need for extensive retroconversion (updating) of data

As you can see from the adjusted scope, there had to be more stakeholders in RDA's development than just librarians. If RDA was going to be meant for the broader metadata community and be based on FRBR/FRAD, the JSC needed to invite participation from groups involved in these areas.

- **FRBR and FRAD** are projects of the International Federation of Library Associations and Institutions (IFLA). FRBR, Functional Requirements for Bibliographic Records, is maintained by the FRBR Review Group. FRAD, Functional Requirements for Authority Data, is overseen by IFLA's Working Group on Functional Requirements and Numbering of Authority Records (FRANAR). The JSC worked closely with these groups to ensure that RDA fully embodied these conceptual models.

- The **DCMI/RDA Task Group** was formed in April 2007 as a result of a meeting between the JSC, the Dublin Core Metadata Initiative (DCMI) and the W3C Semantic Web Deployment Working Group. The metadata community had voiced concerns that AACR3/RDA was not adequately addressing the potential benefits of applying metadata practices to the new cataloging rules. The DCMI/RDA Task Group has worked on defining an RDA Element Vocabulary and registering RDA Value Vocabularies on the Web.

- In early 2008, the **RDA/MARC Working Group** was established to coordinate changes needed in MARC21 as a result of RDA (Schwartz). While many hope that MARC will be replaced by a more versatile, Web-friendly standard, RDA's initial implementation is using MARC21 since almost all library systems and data use it.

- The JSC worked with IFLA in another context. IFLA's Meeting of Experts on an International Cataloging Code (**IME ICC**) has updated the "Paris Principles" (on which AACR is based) in its *Statement on International Cataloguing Principles* (Tillett and Cristán). In recognition that RDA's international scope should coordinate with these principles, the two groups worked together and maintained contact throughout RDA's development.

- Finally, the JSC invited the publishing community to cooperate with them because of their work developing ONIX, a metadata scheme used to describe publisher data. The **RDA/ONIX framework,** which addresses the issues of resource categorization, was released in 2006 ("RDA/ONIX"). RDA (and ONIX) seeks to decouple content designation from carrier designation. What this means in practice is that it tries to provide a more sensible way (in comparison to

AACR2) to describe resource content separately from resource format, for example, maps on microfilm, serials in e-form, or books on CD.

RDA Reorganized: From AACR2 to FRBR

In October 2007, the JSC announced that they were reorganizing the rules to more closely reflect FRBR ("Outcomes" 2007). The original format had mirrored AACR2, with two parts, Description (A) and Access Points (B). The new format arranges content into 10 sections, along FRBR concepts. Sections 1 through 4 deal with FRBR entities (works, expressions, manifestations, items) and sections 5 through 10 deal with FRBR relationships (e.g., work to work, work to expression). This is a major shift for the cataloging community and makes RDA feel very different from AACR2. In some ways this is a good thing, since developers want to encourage new thinking. On the other hand, it requires catalogers to learn a new organization to answer what are essentially the same questions. How do I assign a title? What do I do when there are four authors listed?

LC's Quiet Bombshell

Close on the heels of the decision to reorganize, the Library of Congress Working Group on the Future on Bibliographic Control released its final report in January 2008. Quietly buried within was recommendation 3.2.5 "Suspend work on RDA." The Working Group had convened in November 2006 and met throughout the following year. It was charged to:

- Present findings on how bibliographic control and other descriptive practices can effectively support management of and access to library materials in the evolving information and technology environment;

- Recommend ways in which the library community can collectively move toward achieving this vision;

- Advise the Library of Congress on its role and priorities.

In the end, work was not suspended. The Library of Congress issued another report in June 2008, *Response to On the Record: Report of the Library of Congress Working Group on the Future of Bibliographic Control* (Marcum). In it, LC agreed to continue to participate in the RDA development process, and to test and evaluate it after its release. No promise was made to adopt the new rules.

The final draft of RDA was released in portable document format (pdf) in November 2008. Review of this print draft ended in February 2009. It had been hoped that a review period for the online interface would be possible at the same time, but that did not happen. An open-access trial period for the online product, *RDA Toolkit,* was made available from June through August 2010.

CHAPTER 2

What Is FRBR?
Who Is FRAD?

In October 2007 the Joint Steering Committee announced that it had devised a new organization for RDA. Rather than follow the format of AACR2, RDA would be organized around FRBR and FRAD. FRBR, the Functional Requirements for Bibliographic Records, is pronounced *furber.* FRAD is the Functional Requirements for Authority Data. Both are projects of the International Federation of Library Associations and Institutions (IFLA). The IFLA's Study Group on Functional Requirements for Bibliographic Records began work in 1992 and its final report appeared in 1998. The Working Group on Functional Requirements and Numbering of Authority Records (FRANAR) was established in 1999. Its draft report *Functional Requirements for Authority Data: A Conceptual Model* (FRAD) came out in April 2007 and was approved in March 2009. A Working Group on Functional Requirements for Subject Authority Records (FRSAR) was appointed in 2005 and released its second draft, *Functional Requirements for Subject Authority Data* (FRSAD), in June 2009. Its work will be incorporated into RDA at a later date.

There are three main parts of FRBR and FRAD that are difficult in the abstract but familiar when explained. The easiest way to understand FRBR and FRAD is to concentrate on these main areas. This chapter looks at the first challenge. Chapters 3 and 4 discuss the second and third challenges.

- Challenge One: Learn the lingo, know the vocabulary

- Challenge Two: Get a firm grasp of the group 1 entities in FRBR

- Challenge Three: Understand Relationships

A Conceptual Model

The first challenge when dealing with FRBR and FRAD is the big picture and vocabulary. Most librarians will be unfamiliar with the terms employed. Luckily, once explained, most of the concepts behind the terms will be familiar.

Both FRBR and FRAD are conceptual models for organizing bibliographic and authority information based on the needs of the data's users. Although sometimes you hear them referred to as "data models," they are technically not. Here are some of the descriptions you'll see for FRBR:

- An entity-relationship model (Tillett 2)

- A theoretical model for representing concepts and relationships (Baden 5)

- A vocabulary for specifying levels of representation for bibliographic data (Maurer 2)

- A new model of the bibliographic universe (Maxwell 1)

FRAD calls itself "an extension and expansion of the FRBR model" (FRAD iii) and is likewise a conceptual model built on entity-relationship analysis.

Entity-Relationship Analysis

Both FRBR and FRAD use an entity analysis technique as their primary methodology (FRBR 9; FRAD 2). Entity analysis, or entity-relationship analysis, is an approach used in database design. It first seeks to identify those concepts or objects most important to users in a particular information environment and label them as entities. Relationships between entities are then defined, as are specific characteristics—attributes—for each entity. FRBR defines three entity groups, containing specific types of *entities,* each having a set of *attributes,* and each able to relate to others in a variety of identified *relationships.*

CONCEPTUAL MODELS	FRBR, FRAD, FRSAD
Based on:	ENTITY-RELATIONSHIP MODEL
Made up of:	<ul><li>ENTITIES</li><li>ATTRIBUTES</li><li>RELATIONSHIPS</li></ul>
Focused on:	USER NEEDS
	FRBR <ul><li>Find</li><li>Identify</li><li>Select</li><li>Obtain</li></ul> FRAD <ul><li>Find</li><li>Identify</li><li>Contextualize</li><li>Justify</li></ul>

Figure 1: Summary of Conceptual Model Concepts

Making User Needs Their Focus

Both FRBR and FRAD were charged to design models that specifically relate their data (bibliographic and authority) to user needs.

FRBR identifies the following user tasks (FRBR 79):

■ Find: Find entities that correspond to user's stated search criteria

■ Identify: Confirm that entity corresponds to what is sought

■ Select: Choose an entity that meets user's needs

■ Obtain: To acquire through purchase, loan, electronic access

Because it deals with authority data, FRAD identifies slightly different tasks (FRAD 50):

- Find: Find entities that correspond to user's criteria
- Identify: Confirm that entity corresponds to what is sought
- Contextualize: Place a person, corporate body, work, and so on, in context
- Justify: Document the reason for choosing a name or form of name

FRBR and FRAD (and eventually FRSAD) are not meant to replace AACR2 as a cataloging code, nor MARC as a data format. They are conceptual models for data and not sets of rules. While FRBR identifies "Title" as an entity, it provides no rules for how a cataloger might record a title in a bibliographic record. This will be taken care of in RDA, which uses the models as a beginning point for establishing cataloging rules. In sum, then, FRBR, FRAD, and FRSAD are theoretical models meant to be code- (rules) and system- (format) neutral. Together, FRBR, FRAD, and FRSAD represent a radically new way to think about cataloging. More importantly, they offer the potential to improve our public catalogs and make discovery of resources more rewarding and less frustrating for users.

CHAPTER 3

FRBR and FRAD Entities

The second challenge to understanding FRBR is to understand how entities, especially group 1 entities, work. FRBR divides entities into three groups.

- *Group 1/Primary:* Products of intellectual or artistic endeavor
- *Group 2:* Those responsible for producing group 1 entities
- *Group 3:* Subjects of intellectual or artistic endeavor

This breakdown, once explained, is relatively familiar to librarians. Group 1 entities represent the resources that libraries catalog and make available to users. Group 2 entities represent those who have a hand in the creation and production of group 1 resources, for example, authors, editors, illustrators, producers, publishers, or distributors. Group 3 entities represent the subject analysis done by catalogers to provide access to resources (e.g., subject, name, or geographic headings). The challenge comes in how group 1 entities are defined.

Group 1 Entities: The Promise of WEMI

FRBR's approach to group 1 entities represents a major change and opportunity in approach to bibliographic resources. Group 1 entities differentiate between levels of existence of a resource, identifying conceptual, as well as physical, modes of being. The notion of working with the intellectual content of a work separately from specific instances of it opens exciting and interesting possibilities, especially in the area of discovery and display in the Catalog.

The four levels, or entities, of group 1 are:

- *W*orks
- *E*xpressions
- *M*anifestations
- *I*tems

Works

The first level of bibliographic existence, a work, is defined in FRBR as "a distinct intellectual or artistic creation" (FRBR 17). An abstract notion, it is both the idea and intellectual content that make a work.

EXAMPLE OF A WORK

• Robert McCloskey's *Make Way for Ducklings*

Remember that in FRBR, every entity is further defined by a set of *attributes*. Work-level attributes include title and date of the work. A title serves to identify the work (something to call the idea or intellectual content). A date provides information about when a work's creator formulated her ideas.

Expressions

The second level is an expression, which FRBR defines as "the intellectual or artistic *realization* of a work in the form of alpha-numeric, musical, or choreographic notation, sound, image, object, movement, etc., or any combination of such forms" (FRBR 19). Again, this is more of an abstract notion than a corporeal thing.

EXPRESSIONS OF *MAKE WAY FOR DUCKLINGS*

• The original English text
• Osvaldo Blanco's Spanish translation, *Abran paso a los patitos*
• Rod Ross's spoken reading of McCloskey's English-language words

---

Expression attributes include an expression-level title (perhaps different from the work-level title), language of the expression, and form (the means by which the work is realized, e.g., alpha-numeric notation, spoken word, musical sound).

Manifestations

Things become real at the third bibliographic entity. A manifestation is "the physical embodiment of an expression of a work . . . [and] represents all the physical objects that bear the same characteristics, in respect to both intellectual content and physical form" (FRBR 21).

MANIFESTATIONS OF THE EXPRESSION OF THE WORK *MAKE WAY FOR DUCKLINGS*

- The physical copies of Viking's 1941 publication of the book
- The physical copies of Puffin Books' 1977 publication of the book
- The physical copies of Viking's 1996 Spanish translation
- The physical copies of Weston Woods' 2004 production of the CD that captures Rodd Ross's voice as he reads McCloskey's text

---

Attributes of manifestations include those pieces of information that describe the production of a physical entity. For example, an edition, a publisher or manufacturer, a place of publication, form of carrier (cassette, DVD, microfilm, book), and a variety of physical descriptors for various forms (e.g., type size, playing speed, presentation format, or system requirements).

Items

The final level is an item, which is defined as a single example of a particular manifestation. Attributes of items include an item identifier (e.g., a barcode) and condition of the item (missing pages, damage, autograph).

Exciting Possibilities

As mentioned previously, FRBR's designation of four levels of bibliographic existence opens the door to exciting possibilities for the future of catalogs and cataloging. If one work-level record, and all of its work-level attributes, can be shared by every expression of that work, we might eliminate much of the repetition and redundancy commonly found in cataloging today. Likewise, one expression-level record could suffice for multiple manifestations of that expression. For example, if I have copies of both Viking's 1941 printing and Puffin's 1977 printing

Abstract and Ethereal Realms	WORK	Intellectual content, an idea or concept
	EXPRESSION	Realization of intellectual content in language, sound, musical notation, etc.
Physical and Real Realms	MANIFESTATION	Physical embodiment of an expression of a work, the set of copies (one or many) produced
	ITEM	One particular copy of a manifestation

Figure 2: FRBR Group 1 (Primary) Entities

of *Make Way for Ducklings,* they would share both a work-level record and an expression-level record. Hence, I could use (or point to) the same work- and expression-level records to describe the intellectual content they have in common, and only have to describe their manifestation-level differences in separate manifestation records. This scenario has implications for the public catalog as well. Discovery paths and displays could drill logically down from a listing of works, to expressions, to manifestations, and finally to items.

Group 2 Entities: Responsible for Works

Group 2 entities are those entities responsible for creating, producing, or disseminating group 1 products. FRBR defines two entities: person and corporate body. FRAD adds family to this group. Hence, group 2 entities are:

- Person
  - Defined as "an individual" (FRBR 23)
  - Examples: Ezra Jack Keats, Kate Greenaway
- Corporate body
  - Defined as "an organization or group of individuals and/or organizations acting as a unit" (FRBR 24)
  - Example: Eric Carle Museum of Picture Book Art, Weston Woods Studios

- Family (added by FRAD)
  - Defined as "two or more persons related by birth, marriage, adoption, or similar legal status, or otherwise present themselves as a family" (FRAD 8)
  - Examples: Alcott family, Trapp family, Dukes of Burgundy

Group 3 Entities: Subjects of Works

Group 3 entities identify the subjects of works (FRBR 17). The four defined entities are concept, object, event, and place. These correspond to the kinds of subject headings provided in current catalog records. Some examples from the Library of Congress Subject Headings would be:

- Concept: Adaptability (Psychology)
- Object: Automobiles
- Event: Gettysburg, Battle of, Gettysburg, Pa., 1863
- Place: Plymouth Rock (Plymouth, Mass.)

			Abbreviations for Entities*
Group 1 (Primary)	RESOURCES	Products of intellectual or artistic endeavors	WEMI
Group 2	CREATORS	Those responsible for producing Group One entities	P,F,Cb
Group 3	SUBJECTS	Subjects of intellectual or artistic endeavors	COPE+

Figure 3: Review of FRBR Entities, Groups 1, 2, and 3

* WEMI = Works, Expressions, Manifestations, Items; P,F,Cb = Persons, Families, Corporate Bodies; COPE+ = Concepts, Objects, Places, Events + WEMI + P,F,Cb.

In addition, all group 1 and group 2 entities may also be group 3 entities. This is because group 1 (products of intellectual or artistic endeavor) and group 2 entities (persons, families, corporate bodies) may be the subjects of works, for example, literary criticism of a book or biography of a person.

Hence, group 3 entities are:

- Concept
- Object
- Event
- Place
- Group 1 entities
- Group 2 entities

Functional Requirements for Authority Data (FRAD) Entities

The Functional Requirements for Authority Data (FRAD) is a conceptual model that defines how authority and bibliographic entities are related. In general, authority control seeks to disambiguate and collocate similar titles and names used in bibliographic records by specifying how the title or name should appear and what cross-references should be established. In this way, all titles written by a specific author or all versions of a title can be retrieved together. In current cataloging practice, the headings are referred to as authorized forms and cross-references. FRAD uses a different vocabulary for similar concepts and establishes controlled access points that include both preferred access points (authorized headings) and variant forms. The Library of Congress (LC) Authorities file is a common source for authorized headings. *Gilgamesh* is the authorized form of title in LC Authorities, although the story is also frequently called *The Epic of Gilgamesh*.

The FRAD model has three main blocks. The first block contains the bibliographic entities from FRBR. The second block deals with names and identifiers for the first block entities. The third block describes controlled access points for them.

- Block One: Bibliographic Entities
  - All of the group 1, 2, and 3 FRBR entities are defined as bibliographic entities in FRAD. These are "the entities on which

authority data is focused" (Patton 7). The FRBR entities are work, expression, manifestation, item, person, family, corporate body, concept, object, place, and event.

- Block Two: Name and Identifier Entities

  - *Name:* Each of the entities in block one may be known by one or more names. A name is defined as "a character [e.g., a letter, number, symbol] or group of words and/or characters by which an entity is known" (FRAD 12): *Gone With the Wind* is the name of a work. "Avi" is the name of a person. Note that a specific instance of a bibliographic entity (e.g., a specific person or a specific work) may be known by more than one name. A Pope can be known in various ways (Angelo Giuseppe Roncalli, John XXIII, or Catholic Church Pope). An author can write under various pseudonyms (Dean Koontz, David Axton, or Brian Coffey). Manifestations of a work can go by different titles (e.g., *Beowulf, Story of Beowulf, Aldfrith's Beowulf,* or *Adventures of Beowulf*).

  - *Identifier:* "A number, code, word, phrase, logo, device, etc. that is uniquely identified with an entity" (FRAD 13). An entity from

Bibliographic Entities	● FRBR Entities		
	Group 1: Work Expression Manifestation Item	Group 2: Person Family Corporate Body	Group 3: Concept Object Place Event
Authority Entities	*Known by/Assigned:*		
	● Names ● Identifiers		
	Used to construct:		
	● Controlled Access Points		
	By whom:		*According to what:*
	● Agency		● Rules

Figure 4: FRAD Entities

block one may have several different kinds of unique identifiers (ISBN, publisher number), but each identifier can identify only one entity.

- Block Three: Controlled Access Points

    - *Controlled Access Point:* "A name, term, code, etc. under which a bibliographic or authority record or reference will be found" (FRAD 14). The Library of Congress (LC) Authorities file contains controlled access points, as does the Getty *Art & Architecture Thesaurus (AAT)*.

    - *Rules:* "A set of instructions relating to the formulation and/or recording of controlled access points" (FRAD 15). The LC Authorities are formulated using AACR2 (and shortly RDA). The Getty AAT headings follow Getty's editorial guidelines.

    - *Agency:* "An organization responsible for creating or modifying a controlled access point" (FRAD 15).

CHAPTER 4

FRBR and FRAD Relationships

The third big challenge to understanding FRBR and FRAD is to understand their painstaking explication of the kinds of relationships that can exist between identified entities. This is the crucial second half of developing an entity-relationship model. On a theoretical level, the relationships can be confusing, but when brought down to common sense, they begin to seem familiar. Many already exist in current bibliographic or authority records.

In FRBR, two broad groups of relationships are discussed—logical relationships within or between entity groups and other relationships between group 1 entities.

Logical Relationships in FRBR

Logical relationships between group 1 entities are thus described because the relationship is inherent in the definitions of the entities. For lack of a specified term, I will call these existential relationships.

- A "work" *is realized through* an Expression
- An "expression" *is embodied in* a Manifestation
- A "manifestation" *is exemplified by* an Item

The entities in group 2, person and corporate body, also have logical relationships with group 1 entities. FRBR describes them as responsibility relationships.

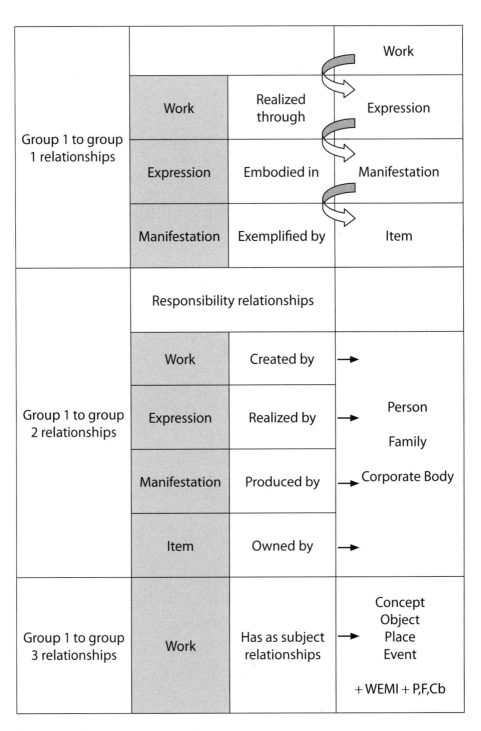

Group 1 to group 1 relationships			Work
	Work	Realized through	Expression
	Expression	Embodied in	Manifestation
	Manifestation	Exemplified by	Item
Group 1 to group 2 relationships	Responsibility relationships		
	Work	Created by	→
	Expression	Realized by	→ Person
			Family
	Manifestation	Produced by	→ Corporate Body
	Item	Owned by	→
Group 1 to group 3 relationships	Work	Has as subject relationships	→ Concept Object Place Event + WEMI + P,F,Cb

Figure 5: FRBR Logical Relationships

- A "work" *is created by* a group 2 entity
- An "expression" *is realized by* a group 2 entity
- A "manifestation" *is produced by* a group 2 entity
- An "item" *is owned by* a group 2 entity

The last of the logical relationships is the *has as its subject* relationship that may exist between a work and any of the group 1, 2, or 3 entities. A work may have as its subject another work, an expression, a manifestation, or an item. A work may also have as its subject a person, family, or corporate body. Finally, a work may have as its subject a concept, object, event, or place.

Other Group 1 Relationships in FRBR

FRBR describes "other" group 1 relationships as those that occur between group 1 entities but are not inherent between them. Section 5.3 in FRBR groups the relationships into nine broad categories of relationships, each of which contains a set of more specific relationship types. Differentiating between the relationships can be confusing. There can seem to be redundancy between relationships at the work or expression levels and relationships at the manifestation and item levels. It helps to keep in mind that works and expressions are not physical things, while manifestations and items are. The relationships are most easily understood by citing, when possible, familiar library situations that demonstrate them.

- Work to Work
    - A work-to-work relationship exists between two separate works. A sequel has a work-to-work relationship with its predecessor. A concordance or supplement has a work-to-work relationship with its main work. A parody has this relationship with the work parodied.
- Whole-to-Part Work-Level Relationship
    - When a part of a work can be described separately, but is still an inherent part of a work, there is a whole/part work-to-work relationship. An example might be a journal issue (the whole work) and one article (a part).
- Expression to Work
    - An expression-to-work relationship is similar to a work-to-work one. For example, an expression of one work can be a parody of a separate work.

- Expression to Expression
  - These relationships may exist between different expressions of the same work or between expressions of separate works. If an expression of a work is abridged slightly, but not enough to be called a new work, the abridged version has an expression-to-expression relationship with its originating expression.

- Manifestation to Manifestation
  - Reproductions of various kinds can represent manifestation-to-manifestation relationships. Digital copies, reprints, facsimiles, and microreproductions are made from specific manifestations of works. They are related to the manifestation because they originate from it.

- Whole-to-Part Manifestation-Level Relationship
  - If a work is manifested in multiple parts (e.g., a presidential biography printed in three volumes), volume one has a part-to-whole relationship with the whole set. While similar to a work-level whole to part relationship, this differs in that the manifestation level deals with the actual physical copies.

- Manifestation to Item
  - This relationship applies when a particular item is used to create a reproduction to be used to produce a manifestation. If a specific item is used to create a facsimile edition (perhaps because of notes taken in the margin by a specific person), this relationship exists.

- Item to Item
  - When one or more items are bound together with each other, or when an item is taken apart and separated into one or more distinct physical units, an item-to-item relationship exists. When a library takes its specific issues of a serial title (its specific items) and binds them together in one volume, the separate issues (items) have an item-to-item relationship with each other.

- Whole-to-Part Item-Level Relationship
  - A whole-to-part item relationship exists in the above example between the single bound volume (an item in your library) and the separate issues it contains (they were also items in your library).

The utility of some of these relationships are self-evident, others may seem overly abstract or unlikely. In defining them, FRBR seeks to identify as many as possible, whether they would be common occurrences or not.

FRAD Relationships

FRAD defines four broad categories of relationships.

- Relationships at the highest level of generalization
- Relationships between persons, families, corporate bodies, and works
- Relationships between names and persons, families, corporate bodies, and works
- Relationships between controlled access points

FRAD's Highest Level Relationships

The highest-level relationships in FRAD are similar to FRBR's logical relationships. They define the relationship between the main groups of entities.

- Bibliographic entities **are known by** at least one, and sometimes more than one, name.
- Bibliographic entities **may be assigned** an identifier. For example, publishers may assign the books they publish unique ISBNs.
- Names and identifiers **are used as the basis for** formulating controlled access points. Controlled access points include both preferred (authorized) headings as well as variant forms of headings (FRAD 14).
- Controlled access points are **governed by** rules. Formulating controlled access points is done using rules such as AACR2 or RDA.
- Rules are **applied by** agencies. Agencies are the organizations that participate in adding, editing, or maintaining headings in a given thesaurus (such as Getty's ATT).
- Agencies **create/modify** controlled access points.

Relationships between Persons, Families, Corporate Bodies, and Works

These relationships occur between the FRBR bibliographic entities found in the first block of the FRAD model. The categories discussed in FRAD are not a complete listing, but they include:

- Relationships between persons
- Relationships between persons and families

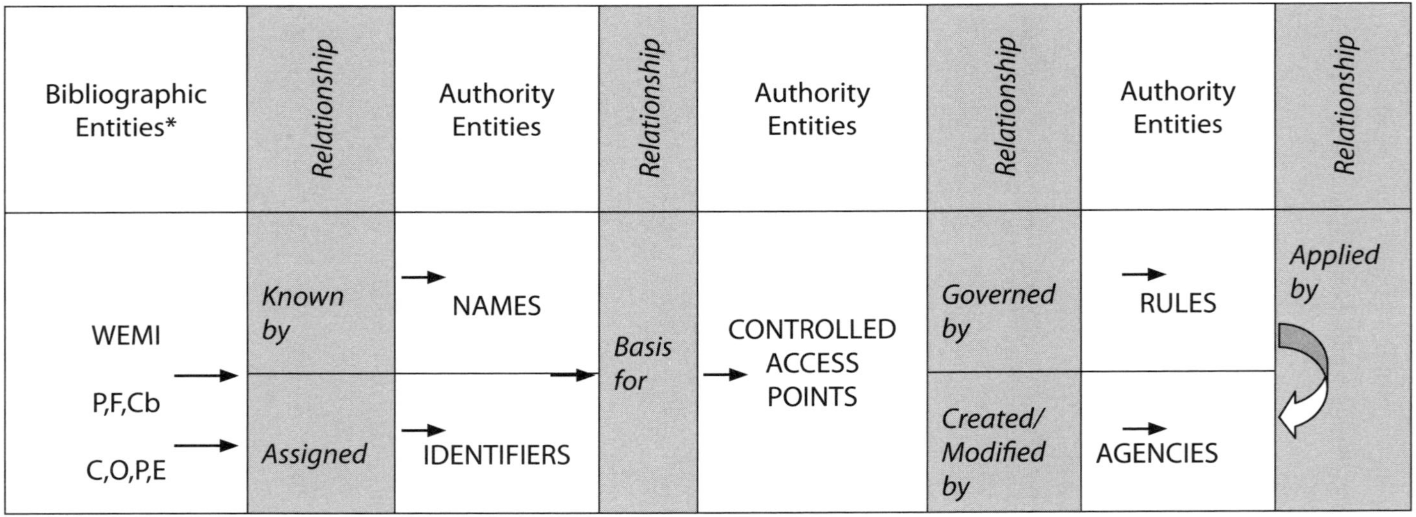

Figure 6: FRAD's Highest Level Relationships

* WEMI = Works, Expressions, Manifestations, Items; P,F,Cb = Persons, Families, Corporate Bodies; C,O,P,E = Concepts, Objects, Places, Events.

- Relationships between persons and corporate bodies
- Relationships between families
- Relationships between corporate bodies
- Relationships between works

As an example, the relationship between a person (Bill Gates) and a corporate body (Microsoft) is brought out in a source data note in LC Authorities. This is current practice and will likely be continued with RDA's initial implementation.

Relationships between Names and Persons, Families, Corporate Bodies, and Works

These relationships are called "known by" relationships because they relate the FRBR entities from block one with the names by which they are known—the name entities from block two. The broad categories of relationships are between:

- Persons and names
- Families and names
- Corporate bodies and names
- Works and names

International Business Machines offers an example of a corporate body-to-name relationship. The company is known both by its full name and by an acronym (IBM). Both names represent the same corporate body, demonstrating that a specific entity may have one or more forms of name. This kind of relationship is sometimes expressed using "see" or "see also" references in today's authority structures.

Relationships between Controlled Access Points

This category looks at the entities in the third block of the FRAD model. Relationships here occur between controlled access points. The most common will be:

- Parallel language relationships (access points for the same entity given in different language[s])
- Alternate script relationships (access points for the same entity given in a language that uses a different alphabet or script, such as Chinese or Russian)

- Different rules relationships (access points for the same entity but formulated following different rules). In LC, the authorized form for the city of Indianapolis is "Indianapolis (Ind.)." In Getty's *Thesaurus of Geographic Names* the preferred form is "Indianapolis." These headings have a different rules relationship.

Conclusion

FRBR, FRAD, and FRSAD (still in draft) are theoretical models for library data. When the JSC decided to structure the new cataloging rules on them, they took a bold step forward. As we will see in the next chapter, RDA is thoroughly based on FRBR and FRAD, with placeholders for FRSAD. Successful implementation of RDA will encourage further investigation into using these data models, which could lead to new, more versatile, structures for our bibliographic and authority data. A word of caution, however. While many librarians and catalogers believe that FRBR and FRAD are steps in the right direction, the path to their realization is unclear. If we have redesigned resource description structures, will we also need redesigned library systems? What will happen to our legacy data, in MARC format? Despite these questions, the models hold great promise for improving catalogs and cataloging.

CHAPTER 5

AACR2 to RDA

RDA can be more challenging at a macro rather than micro level. At the higher level, the models, concepts, and vocabulary are very different from AACR2 and can be a little off-putting. Once you get into specific rules, because of RDA's goal of backward compatibility, things look more familiar.

To help with the bigger picture, this chapter begins with a look at how RDA's vocabulary has its roots in FRBR and FRAD. It then draws parallels between AACR2 and RDA terms, giving equivalents and identifying changes in concepts. From there, the chapter builds a bridge from AACR2 to RDA by comparing the structure of the former with the latter.

FRBR/FRAD-Based Vocabulary and Concepts

Elements and the RDA Element Set

Although not given much fanfare in RDA itself, the term "element" plays a more important role in RDA than it did in AACR2. While AACR2 refers to ISBD (G) elements, and RDA retains AAR2's definition of element in its glossary, element and element set are also terms used in the metadata community. To some extent, use of the term in RDA reflects its goal to design a cataloging code for the digital, as well as analog, environment.

It is also important to understand that the RDA elements correspond to the attributes and relationships delineated in FRBR and FRAD. As described in RDA's introductory chapter:

> RDA is divided into ten sections: sections 1–4 cover *elements corresponding to the entity attributes* defined in FRBR and FRAD; sections 5–10 cover *elements corresponding to the relationships* defined in FRBR and FRAD. (Italics mine; RDA 0.5)

The RDA Element Set, then, is the complete collection of terms devised to correspond to FRBR or FRAD attributes and relationships, as well as some additional elements not present in FRBR or FRAD but unique to RDA.

New Terms, Altered Concepts

AACR2 follows the General International Standard Bibliographic Description ISBD (G) and divides the bibliographic description into areas. There is a title and statement of responsibility area, an edition area, and so on. In RDA, areas become elements, and there is a title element, statement of responsibility element, edition element, and so on. RDA's elements do not appear in ISBD (G) order.

RDA also jettisons the AACR2 terms main and added entry in favor of the more inclusive label access points. RDA uses the term preferred access point rather than authorized heading. A name authority heading is

AACR2 Concept and Term	RDA Concept and Term
Areas (e.g., Title area)	Elements (e.g., Title elements)
Main Entry Added Entries	Access Points
Authorized Heading	Preferred Access Point
Name Authority	Preferred Name
Uniform Title	Preferred Title
See/See also References	Variant Access Point, Variant Name, or Variant Title for a Work
Chief Source of Information	Preferred Source of Information

Figure 7: AACR2 versus RDA Vocabulary

a preferred name. Uniform titles become preferred titles. Other forms of headings are called variant access points, with both variant titles and variant names possible. In a similar vein, the chief source of information in AACR2 is called the preferred source of information in RDA.

RDA Structure

RDA's structure is fundamentally FRBR-ized. The first four sections deal with the attributes of FRBR/FRAD entities while sections 5 through 10 deal with FRBR/FRAD relationships. While not explicitly labeled parts 1 and 2 in RDA, I will, at times, refer to the two groups of sections in this way. RDA's structure has the following features:

- Aligned with conceptual models for FRBR and FRAD
  - Intended to cover and support all types of content and media, including digital
  - Flexible and extensible to adopt to new technologies and formats
- Two parts: 10 sections; introduction + 37 chapters
  - **[Part 1] Attributes:** sections 1–4; chapters 1–16
  - **[Part 2] Relationships:** sections 5–10; chapters 17–37
- Online format: RDA's co-publishers believe that RDA is best presented and used in an online environment. Although they announced in April 2010 that a print version would be produced, they encourage libraries to consider the online product, *RDA Toolkit,* as the preferred interface.

AACR2 Structure

AACR2 has two parts: part 1, "Description," and part 2, "Headings, Uniform Titles, and References." Part 1 lays out rules for creating the descriptive part of a catalog record. It follows ISBD (G), International Standard Book Description (General), which prescribes the order of elements and their punctuation. Chapter 1 provides general rules that apply to all library materials. Subsequent chapters discuss rules for specific formats (books, sound recordings, serials, etc.).

Part 2 deals with the choice of main entry, added entries, and references (e.g., see, see also). Rules for including and formatting headings for names, geographic places, corporate bodies, and uniform titles are given.

RDA and AACR2: Part 1

Like part 1 of AACR2, RDA's first grouping of sections includes rules for the descriptive part of a catalog record. The sections tell how to describe entities (works, expressions, manifestations, items) using their designated elements (attributes). Since RDA's elements largely overlap with AACR2's descriptive areas (title, statement of responsibility, physical description), much of what is covered in part 1 of AACR2 can also be found in this first part of RDA. However, it may be found in a completely different place.

In AACR2, part 1, chapters are organized around formats. Chapter 1 provides general rules for describing a resource. For rules pertaining to specific formats (e.g., books, manuscripts, sound recordings, motion pictures), one consults separate chapters.

In contrast, corresponding sections of RDA are organized around the four group 1 entities (works, expressions, manifestations, and items). Instructions for recording attributes of manifestations and items are given in section 1 (chapters 1–4). Instructions for recording attributes of works and expressions are given in section 2 (chapters 5–7). Within each chapter, general instructions are given for each element. Instructions for specific formats are included here. For example, in chapter 2, Rule 2.3.4.3 provides general guidelines on how to record other title information. A few rules down, Rule 2.3.4.5 offers specific information on providing other title information for cartographic resources.

While RDA keeps rules pertaining to special formats together under their entity element, it does parse rules out among entities. This can lead to separating things that we are used to finding together. A good example occurs in what AACR2 calls the Physical Description area, which includes the extent of an item (e.g., number of pages for a book), other physical details (e.g., illustrative matter), and dimensions. In RDA, the first and third of these, extent and dimensions, are considered elements of a manifestation. As such, rules on how to record them are given in section 1, chapter 3, "Describing Carriers" (for manifestations and items). However, illustrative content is considered an element of a work or expression, and its rules are presented in section 2, chapter 7, "Describing Content" (for works and expressions).

Another difference between AACR2 and RDA is that while AACR2 does not deal with subject headings (except for geographic names), RDA will. Because FRBR and FRAD treat subjects as group 3 entities (concept, object, event, place), RDA includes them in section 4, "Recording Attributes of Concept, Object, Event, and Place." Four of the five chapters in this section have not been written and will not be included in RDA's initial release. They will be added after work is finished on the Functional Requirements for Subject Authority Data (FRSAD). For initial implementation of RDA, one expects that subject headings will be assigned in the current manner, using one of the existing thesauri (Library of Congress, Sears, Medical Subject Headings [MESH]).

RDA and AACR2: Part 2

The second part of RDA is very different from part 2 of AACR2. The second part of RDA explicates the types of relationships possible

AACR2	RDA
Part 1: "Description"	**[Part 1]: "Attributes"**
—Separate chapters on different formats	—All formats treated together
	—Detailed information on formatting name and corporate body headings
	—Subject entities included
Part 2: "Headings"	**[Part 2]: "Relationships"**
—Detailed information on formatting name and corporate body headings	<Moved to part 1>
—Subjects as access points not included	
—Rules for making references explicit. Relationships inferred from references.	—Relationships explicit. References used to express them.
Appendices: 3 + Glossary	**Appendices**: 12 + Glossary
Print format: 26 chapters: 600–700 pages	**Online format**: 10 sections/37 chapters: (draft text = 1,400 + pdf pages)

Figure 8: AACR2 versus RDA Structure

between RDA entities. It focuses on recording relationships rather than constructing headings. Part 2 of AACR2 concentrates on constructing headings. Relationships are touched on tangentially and only as they pertain to making references. This leads to a final difference between AACR2 and RDA. While guidelines for forming headings are presented in part 2 of AACR2, they are largely covered in the first part of RDA. In some ways, then, much of AACR2 fits into the Attributes section of RDA.

Changes from AACR2 to RDA

RDA makes some significant breaks with AACR2. In this chapter, we'll discuss the changes to general principles and how they affect everyday cataloging and resource description. The specific changes we'll cover are the following:

- Principles and objectives are spelled out in RDA
- Clear line of separation between data content and presentation
- Core elements instead of levels of description
- Break from "classes of material" approach
- Different attitude toward transcription of data
- Less use of abbreviations
- Relationships are prominent
- Rule of Three is the exception, not the rule
- Content *and* carrier instead of GMD

Principles and Objectives

In contrast to AACR2 where the Paris Principles of 1961 are cited as guidance but no further discussion of principles is offered, RDA cites the IME-ICC *Statement of International Cataloguing Principles* and explicates the specific principles and objectives followed during RDA development (RDA 0.4).

RDA's objectives are listed in the introductory chapter, section 0.4.2.

- *Responsiveness to User Needs:* Resource descriptions should meet user needs as defined in FRBR and FRAD. Users should be able to find, identify, select, and obtain a resource. In addition, the description should enable users to understand the relationships that exist between the resource, other resources, and the names associated with it.

- *Cost Efficiency:* Resource description should be done in a cost-efficient manner, while supporting user needs.

- *Flexibility:* Data should be format-, medium-, and system-neutral, and able to be used in multiple environments.

- *Continuity:* Data created using RDA should be compatible with existing data (especially AACR2 data).

The principles employed in forming the new catalog code are explained in section 0.4.3.

- *Differentiation:* This principle states that resource and entity descriptions should differentiate the resource or entity from others. The information in a bibliographic record should uniquely describe the resource. The access point constructed for a preferred name should differentiate it from others.

- *Sufficiency:* A resource description should sufficiently describe the resource for the needs of the user.

- *Relationships:* A resource description should indicate its significant relationships to other resources. Access points associated with a resource should also reflect significant relationships.

- *Representation:* This principle reads: "The data describing a resource should reflect the resource's representation of itself" (RDA 0.4.3.4). It goes on to explain that the choice of preferred title and names used in a description should reflect forms commonly used to refer to these entities.

- *Accuracy:* When necessary to provide an accurate resource description, supplementary information should be provided (for example, the inclusion of a note to correct misleading information).

- *Attribution:* Information about persons, families, or corporate bodies associated with a resource should come from the resource itself or from reference sources.

- *Language Preference:* Preferred names should be given in the original language of the resource or in the language of the cataloging agency. Titles should be given in the language of the cataloging agency when a commonly used title is available.

- *Common Usage or Practice:* The principle begins: "Data that is not transcribed from the resource itself should reflect common usage" (RDA 0.4.3.8). Specifically, the choice of first element for a preferred name (person or family) should follow the practice of the country and language with which they are most closely associated.

- *Uniformity:* This principle advocates using RDA's appendices for the purpose of establishing uniform data entry for such things as capitalization and abbreviations.

Separation of Content and Presentation (RDA 0.1)

AACR2 is explicitly tied to the International Standard Book Description (ISBD). Following both its order of elements and prescribed punctuation is required. In RDA, the recording of data is separate from its presentation. RDA deals with recording data only, although it offers guidelines for presentation in appendices. An indication of this difference is found in a comparison of AACR2 and RDA examples.

AACR2

Example for rule 1.1F. Statement of responsibility. Example includes ISBD punctuation:
All that jazz [gmd] / Fats Waller.

RDA

In contrast, at rule 2.4.1.4, Recording Statements of Responsibility, the example shows no formatting:
Fats Waller

Core Elements (RDA 0.6)

Where AACR2 offered three levels of bibliographic description, each successively more full, RDA opts to define a set of Core Elements for each kind of RDA entity. Core elements are identified for resource descriptions of the group 1 entities (manifestations, items, works, and expressions) and for records representing group 2 entities (persons, families, corporate bodies). In addition, core elements are listed for the various types of relationships, including group 1's primary relationships, group 1 to group 2 relationships (resource to person, family, corporate body), and group 3 (subject) relationships.

Break from "Classes of Material" Approach

Part 1 of AACR2 begins with generic rules for describing "all library materials" and then moves on to separate chapters on specific types of materials. In RDA, specific rules for specific types of materials are included in the body of the rules. For example, in chapter 2, the rules for devised titles include the main rule at 2.3.11.3, which you would use for most materials. Specific rules for certain types of materials (music, maps, moving images, and archives) are provided when additional information and guidance is needed.

RULE 2.3.11 DEVISED TITLES

2.3.11.3	Recording Devised Titles *[general rules]*
2.3.11.4	Devised Titles *for Music*
2.3.11.5	Devised Titles *for Cartographic Resources*
2.3.11.6	Devised Titles *for Moving Image Resources*
2.3.11.7	Devised Titles *for Archival Resources and Collections*

Transcription of Data

RDA takes a different approach to transcription than does AACR2. In section 1.7.9, RDA holds that data should generally be recorded as it appears. Hence, if there is a spelling error in a publisher's name as it appears on an item, RDA advises to transcribe the publisher as it appears. If the error is serious enough, a note of clarification may be added. If an error occurs in a title, a variant title may be added with corrected spelling. In contrast, in AACR2, rule 1.0F says to transcribe the inaccuracy followed by "[sic]" or "i.e." and a correction.

AACR2

Breakfast at the red bruck [i.e. brick] house

RDA

Breakfast at the red bruck house

(Variant Title): Breakfast at the red brick house

Less Use of Abbreviations

RDA moves away from using abbreviations in the resource description and favors spelling things out. For instance, instead of using the Latin abbreviation *s.l.* to indicate that no probable place of publication is available, RDA will use "place of publication not identified." When describing the extent (physical description) of a book, words like pages, illustrations, color, and portraits will all be spelled out rather than abbreviated as p., ill., col, and ports.

AACR2

[32] p. : ill. ; 19 cm.

RDA

1 volume (unpaged) : illustrations ; 19 cm

Relationship Designators

Given that RDA is built on FRBR and FRAD, conceptual models built on entity-relationship analysis, it makes sense that relationships play a crucial role in it—indeed, taking up all of its second part. In AACR2, relationships were not emphasized. Rule 21.0D offers an *option* to add a function designation for compilers, editors, illustrators, or translators. However, the rule was optional and very limited.

RDA places as much importance on relationships as it does on description. Sections 5 through 10 provide guidelines on recording relationships, while accompanying appendices provide the terms to be used to describe them.

- Appendix I: Relationships between a resource and persons, families, and corporate bodies associated with a resource

- Appendix J: Relationships between works, expressions, manifestations, and items
- Appendix K: Relationships between persons, families, and corporate bodies
- Appendix L: Relationships between concepts, objects, events, and places (placeholder, to be developed in future releases of RDA)

Rule of Three an Option, Not the Rule

The "Rule of Three" appears throughout AACR2 as a means to limit the number of added entries made for a particular work. In general, the rule instructs that when there are three or more potential access points, to record the first and leave the rest out. This rule is invoked in rule 21.6.B and C for authors and in 21.7B for collective works. RDA tries to be more inclusive and encouraging of multiple access points. It more often recommends including multiple names or titles, and provides *an option* to limit to the first listed.

The Rule of Three may also be seen in parts of the bibliographic description in AACR2. Rule 1.1F5 stated that when more than three names were listed on a resource, only the first name should be recorded in the statement of responsibility. In RDA, rule 2.4.1.5 calls for recording all names in a single statement of responsibility. It offers an "Optional Omission" to list only the first name and summarize what is omitted. This change follows RDA's principle of transcribing information as it appears on the resource.

AACR2

/ by Cornelius Snap ... [et al.]

RDA

by Dr. Cornelius Snap, Michael Crackle, Robert Pop, Jr., and Rice Krispies

---

Content and Carrier Instead of GMD

RDA eliminates the General Material Designator (GMD). The GMD is the sometimes useful, sometimes misleading, term appearing in square brackets after a title.

There have been problems with the GMD because it sometimes describes the form of carrier for, and at other times describes the type of

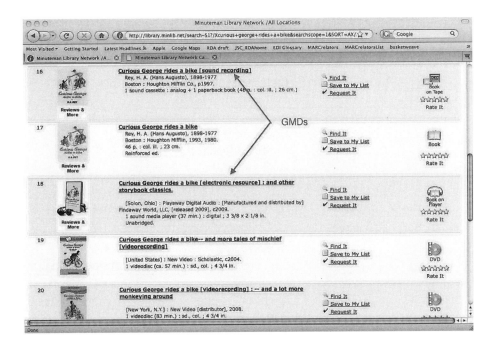

Figure 9: General Material Designation in a Public Catalog Display

content of, a resource. For instance, an audiobook, available on an mp3 or other player device, could be considered a sound recording (its content) or an electronic resource (its carrier). Unfortunately, the GMD did not accommodate both aspects of the material.

The GMD/SMD Working Group was appointed by the JSC to investigate solutions to this issue. They recommended discarding the GMD and using three elements, content type, media type, and carrier type to more fully and accurately describe resources.

AACR2

Title field: Split image [sound recording]

RDA

Title field: Split image
Content Type: Spoken word
Media Type: Audio
Carrier Type: Audio Disc

AACR2 Rule	AACR2 Content	RDA Content	RDA Rule
Title Proper			
1.0F	Some of my pomes [sic]	Some of my pomes (with Variant Title for: Some of my poems)	1.7.9 2.3.6
1.0F	Breakfast at the red bruck [i.e. brick] house	Breakfast at the red bruck house (with Variant Title for: Breakfast at the red brick house)	1.7.9 2.3.6
Statement of Responsibility			
1.1F7	by Harry Chaplin	by Harry Chaplin, Jr.	2.4.1.4
1.1F7	by Barry Pinkwater	by Dr. Barry Pinkwater	2.4.1.4
		by Barry Pinkwater	2.4.1.4 optional omission
1.1F5	by Cornelius Snap . . . [et al.]	by Dr. Cornelius Snap, Michael Crackle, Robert Pop, Jr., and Rice Krispies	2.4.1.5 No more Rule of 3
		by Cornelius Snap [and three others]	2.4.1.5 optional omission
Edition Statement			
1.2B1 App. B	3rd ed. *Title page reads: Third edition*	Third edition *Title page reads: Third edition*	2.5.1.4
Publication, Distributor, etc.			
1.4C5	London; New York *Title page reads: London, Montreal, New York. (U.S. cataloging agency)*	London; Montreal; New York *Title page reads: London, Montreal, New York*	2.8.2.4
1.4C6 1.4D6 1.4F7	[S.l.]: [s.n.], [ca. 1960]	Place of publication not identified Publisher not identified Date of publication not identified	2.8.2.6 2.8.4.7 2.8.6.6
Physical Description (Extent)			
2.5B7	[32] p.	32 unnumbered pages (or) approximately 32 pages (or) 1 volume (unpaged)	3.4.5.3 (three choices)
2.5C	ill.	illustrations	7.15
2.5D	19 cm.	19 cm	3.5.1.4.14

Figure 10: AACR2 and RDA Cataloging Compared

The JSC also worked with the publishing industry, developers of the ONIX metadata scheme for exchanging publishing data (including carrier descriptions), and agreed on an RDA/ONIX framework that both groups can use. Down the road, this will encourage electronic transfer of data between publishers and libraries, thereby reducing duplication of effort.

Conclusion

RDA introduces some big changes in objectives, principles, and approach for cataloging that result in big and small changes in practice. Because its principles are applied across the board in a consistent manner changes in practice are also applied logically. It is easy to see some of the changes at work in even an uncomplicated cataloging record. The developers of RDA hope that these changes will improve the catalog and provide a better discovery experience to users.

CHAPTER 7

MARC Changes

RDA is designed to be both flexible and extensible. It is not solely intended for MARC 21 encoding. Metadata (created using RDA's rules) can also be expressed in other metadata schema, including MODS (LC's Metadata Object Description Schema) and the Dublin Core Metadata Element Set ("RDA Brochure"). That said, initial implementation of RDA for most U.S. libraries will be in MARC 21 to ensure compatibility with our legacy data and existing library systems. This chapter looks at some of the changes approved by the MARC Advisory Committee to enable MARC encoding of RDA data for bibliographic and authority records. Mapping MARC 21 to RDA is covered in appendix D, section D.3, for bibliographic data and in appendix E, section E.3, for authority data. The changes made in MARC 21 to accommodate RDA are described in the Library of Congress MARC Standards Web page "RDA in MARC: January 2010" (http://www.loc.gov/marc/RDAinMARC29. html).

Bibliographic Format: Content, Media, and Carrier Changes

In the bibliographic format, the biggest change in MARC is the introduction of three new fields to accommodate the content, media, and carrier elements in RDA.

336 Content Type

Content type is an element at the work/expression level that describes what the content of a resource is and how it is expressed and perceived. The element represents the "fundamental form of communication in which the content is expressed and the human sense through which it is intended to be perceived" (RDA 6.10). Examples of content type are spoken word, performed music, text, two-dimensional moving image, and computer program. A book (or the work expressed in text and manifested in a book) receives the content type "text." A work expressed in spoken words and manifested as an audiobook on CD is content type "spoken word." A musical work available on CD has content type "performed music." The RDA content type element will be encoded in the MARC 21 field 336. It can be entered as text, using the terms listed in RDA at 6.10.1.3, or it may be entered in coded form. Codes for the terms were established in MARC Update 10 and are available at http://www.loc.gov/marc/list/contentcodes.html.

337 Media Type

Media type is a manifestation/item level element that describes the category of device needed to experience the content of the resource. It is meant to be broader than carrier and is defined as "the general type of intermediation device required to view, play, run, etc., the content of a resource" (RDA 3.2.1.2). A book receives the term "unmediated" as media type, while a movie on DVD is given the term "video." Other examples of media type include audio, computer, and microform. Media type is a more general, bucket-like categorization than carrier. The RDA media type element will be encoded in the MARC 21 field 337, as textual terms (listed in RDA at section 3.2, table 3.1), or as codes (established in MARC Update 10, see http://www.loc.gov/marc/list/mediacodes.html).

338 Carrier Type

Carrier type is also a manifestation/item level element that is more specific than media type. It is meant to describe the specific physical container through or in which a resource's content is packaged or delivered. The element is used to describe "the storage medium and housing of a carrier in combination with the type of intermediation device required to view, play, run, etc., the content of a resource" (RDA 3.3.1.1). The carrier type describes the physical apparatus that contains the artistic or intellectual content of a resource. It is the packaging that carries or conveys the content. Where media type may be broadly set at "video," the carrier type will specify "videocassette" or "videodisc." Some examples of carrier type terms are audio disc, online resource, computer disc, microfilm reel, slide, videocassette, and volume (for a book). The RDA carrier type

	BOOK	DVD	Music CD	Audiobook on CD	Streaming Video
336 subfield a CONTENT term	Text	Two-dimensional moving image	Performed music	Spoken word	Two-dimensional moving image
337 subfield a MEDIA term	Unmediated	Video	Audio	Audio	Video
338 subfield a CARRIER term	Volume	Videodisc	Audio disc	Audio disc	Online resource

Figure 11: Content, Media, and Carrier Terms for Various Resources

element will be encoded in the MARC 21 field 338. As with content and media, carrier may be expressed as a term (see RDA 3.3.1.2) or as a code (see MARC Code List for Carrier Types, http://www.loc.gov/marc/list/carriercodes.html).

Input Conventions for 336, 337, and 338

Each of these fields is repeatable so that if a resource consists of more than one type of content, media, or carrier, as many terms as are necessary may be added. Subfield "a" of these fields contains the actual descriptive term. Subfield "b" contains the coded value representing the term. For all three, the field should contain either a term or a code, but should not contain both a term and its corresponding code.

Theory into Practice

Figure 11 shows how content, media, and carrier terms might be assigned for various formats of materials.

Bibliographic Format: 007 and 008

Additional codes have also been added for the 007 (Physical Description Fixed Field) and 008 (Fixed-Length Data Elements) to represent RDA terms not formerly present in the MARC format. The 007 field contains a string of codes that specify details of the physical characteristics of a resource. Its second code represents the special material designation. There are several new codes here. For example, for electronic resources, the new code "d" is for disc. For nonprojected graphics, there are additional codes "k" for poster, "p" postcard, and "q" icon. The 008 field is a 40-character coded field that provides general information about the resource as a whole. It has three new codes for format of music. The new terms are found in RDA in Rule 7.20.13 (for describing content) and in 3.4.3.2 (for describing the extent) of notated music.

Code h: Chorus Score

Code i: Condensed Score

Code j: Performer-Conductor part

Name-to-Resource Relationships

Section 6, chapters 18–22, of RDA deals with relationships between group 2 entities (persons, families, corporate bodies) and group 1 entities (works, expressions, manifestations, and items). Appendix I provides terms to describe each type of relationship. Appendix I terms will be recorded in subfield "e" in the controlled access fields (1XX, 6XX, 7XX, 8XX) of the MARC 21 bibliographic format, and in the 1XX, 4XX, and 5XX of the authority format. Catalogers may opt to enter relator codes rather than terms, using subfield "4." Codes are found in the MARC Relator Codes list (http://www.loc.gov/marc/relators/relacode.html).

As an example, the abridged audiobook of Leo Tolstoy's *War and Peace*, read by Neville Jason and abridged by Heather Godwin, would have added entries as shown here.

RELATIONSHIP DESIGNATORS: NAME (GROUP 2) TO RESOURCE (GROUP 1) ENTITIES

100	$a Tolstoy, Leo
245	$a War and peace
700	$a Jason, Neville, $e narrator
700	$a Godwin, Heather, $e abridger

Resource-to-Resource Relationships

Section 8, chapters 24–28, of RDA provides guidelines on recording relationships between the group 1 entities. Appendix J lists the terms used for describing these relationships. MARC Update 10 defines subfield "i" in MARC bibliographic 7XX fields and authority 4XX and 5XX fields to indicate these resource-to-resource relationships.

For example, the title *Pride and Prejudice and Zombies* by Seth Grahame-Smith is related to Jane Austen's *Pride and Prejudice* by virtue of being a parody of the original work. Using the appropriate term from RDA's appendix J and applying MARC 21 coding yields the following heading:

RELATIONSHIP DESIGNATORS: GROUP 1 ENTITIES

100	$a Grahame-Smith, Seth
245	$a Pride and prejudice and zombies
700	$i parody of (work) $a Austen, Jane, $d 1775–1817. $t Pride and prejudice.

In addition, the definition of subfield "i" will also be adjusted for the linking fields 76X–78X to allow the use of appendix J relationship designators when needed. Subfield "4" in 760–787 fields will be defined to hold relationship codes, and linking field 787 will be renamed from "Nonspecific Relationship Entry" to "Other Relationship" to allow for relationships not defined in the 760–785 fields. These fields are often used in serials cataloging to link previous and continuing titles to each other.

Authority Format: Name-to-Name Relationships

Section 9, chapters 29–32, of RDA lays out rules for expressing relationships between group 2 entities (i.e., relationships between persons, families, and corporate bodies). Catalogers will refer to appendix K for terms to specify particular relationships. These relationships are mainly expressed in authority records. MARC Update 10 defines subfield "i" so that terms from appendix K may be added as relationship designators in the 4XX and 5XX fields of authority records. Subfield "4" can be used to express the relationships in coded form. (Code "r" in subfield "w" provides user display instructions when subfield "i" or "4" is used.)

AUTHORITY FORMAT: RELATIONSHIP DESIGNATORS IN 5XX SUBFIELD "I"

100	$a Bell, Currer, $d 1816–1855.
500	$w r $i real identity $a Bronte, Charlotte, $d 1816–1855
110	$a Ford Motor Company.
500	$w r $i founder $a Ford, Henry, $d 1863–1947

Subfield "4" will be added to the 4xx and 5xx fields of the authority format to enable the recording of coded data.

Additional MARC Fields for Name and Resource Attributes

A group of fields has been added to the authority format to accommodate new RDA elements for group 2 entities—persons, families, and corporate bodies. Among them are address (field 371), field of activity (field 372), occupation (field 374), and gender (field 375).

There will also be fields added to both the bibliographic and authority formats to cover RDA elements for works and expressions. The 380 field provides a place to record the form of a work (RDA 6.3), which is defined as the class or genre to which a work belongs. It is used to differentiate two works from one another when they share the same title. The RDA elements "Other Distinguishing Characteristics of a Work" and "Other Distinguishing Characteristics of an Expression" (RDA 6.6 and 6.13) will be recorded in the 381 field.

A full list of new authority and bibliographic fields can be found at the Library of Congress's MARC Standards Web page at http://www. loc.gov/marc/RDAinMARC29.html (MARC 21).

Conclusion

With the approval of these MARC changes, RDA is poised to support a smooth transition from AACR2 to RDA. Catalogers can adopt RDA and implement the new rules in a MARC environment.

CHAPTER 8

Putting It All Together

We've looked at RDA's vocabulary and structure, at what has changed from AACR2 to RDA, and at MARC changes made to accommodate RDA's initial implementation. This chapter looks at what it might be like to catalog using RDA. We'll concentrate on part 1 of RDA and look at describing a resource (title, statement of responsibility, edition, publication statement, physical characteristics) rather than on forming headings and authority work. Imagine that you have a resource in hand and that you want to catalog using RDA. After scanning chapter 0 (zero), RDA's introduction, you move into part 1, "Attributes."

RDA Attributes [Part 1]: Table of Contents and Structure

The "Attributes" part of RDA has four sections.

1. Recording attributes of manifestations and items

2. Recording attributes of works and expressions

3. Recording attributes of persons, family, and corporate body

4. Recording attributes of concept, objects, events, and places

The first thing to notice is that RDA begins the cataloging process with manifestations and items. This makes practical sense because our current cataloging practice begins here. We are either ordering a specific manifestation of a title or have received it already when we start cataloging. Section 2 moves on to recording attributes of works and expressions. Section 3 considers the group 2 entities of RDA—those responsible for or involved with the creation and production of a resource. Finally, section 4 provides guidelines for group 3 entities of RDA, the subjects of resources. We will look at section 1 and a portion of section 2.

Section 1: Attributes of Manifestation and Item

As noted, RDA begins the cataloging process with describing manifestations and items. Section 1 contains four chapters:

- General Guidelines on Recording Attributes of Manifestations and Items
- Identifying Manifestations and Items
- Describing Carriers
- Providing Acquisitions and Access Information

Section 1: Chapter 1: General Guidelines

Chapter 1 begins with an explanation of terminology, including definitions for types of descriptions and modes of issuance.

Description types:

- A *comprehensive* description describes a resource as a whole
- An *analytical* description catalogs a part of a resource
- A *hierarchical* description combines the two

Mode of issuance is defined with four options:

- A resource issued and described as a single unit
- A multipart monograph
  - This term applies to both print and nonprint resources
- A serial, a resource issued in successive parts, intending to run indefinitely
- An integrating resource, a resource wherein content may be updated and changed regularly, for instance, a Web site where new data is added on a regular basis.

Section 1: Chapter 2: Identifying Manifestations and Items

Chapter 2 begins with a discussion of how to choose a source of information to use in creating a resource description. In AACR2, the term "chief source of information" was defined as the source to be preferred and consulted first when preparing a bibliographic description. In RDA, the same concept is described as the "preferred source of information." The preferred source of information is the place from which you prefer to determine a resource's title, author, publication details, and so on. (If the preferred source fails to provide necessary information, other sources—as described in section 2.2.4—can be consulted.)

The preferred source is based on the type of description (comprehensive, analytical, hierarchical) and mode of issuance of a resource, as well as on the type (or format) of the resource. Here are the three possible formats and their preferred sources:

- For resources consisting of pages, leaves, sheets, or cards (or images of the same)—the preferred source of information will be a title page, title sheet, or title card.

- For resources consisting of moving images—the preferred source is a title frame or screen.

- For other resources—a permanently fixed or printed label, or embedded textual metadata—that provide a title should be used.

Once a preferred source of information is identified, chapter 2 proceeds through most of the elements (attributes) that pertain to a manifestation or item. The following list covers the basic elements for manifestations (core elements are marked with asterisks). Core elements are required only when applicable to a given resource, so they don't have to be included in every resource description.

- Title proper (and additional title subelements such as earlier and variant title)*
  - The title proper is the title chosen as the chief name of a resource
- Statement of responsibility*
- Edition statement*
- Numbering of serials*

- Publication, or distribution, or manufacture statements
  - Place
  - Name*
  - Date *
- Copyright date*
- Series statement*
- Identifier for the manifestation (ISBN, ISSN)*
- Notes (multiple elements for specific notes)

Section 1: Chapter 3: Describing Carriers

Missing from chapter 2 are those elements that describe the physical characteristics of a manifestation or item. These elements are found in chapter 3 "Describing Carriers." Carrier type is a core element. Other elements may be included when appropriate to the type of material being cataloged. Some of the more familiar carrier characteristics include:

- Media type
- Carrier type*
- Extent (*core if complete extent is known)
- Dimensions
- Reduction ratio (of microimages)
- Sound characteristics
- Projection characteristics of motion picture film
- Video characteristics
- Digital file characteristics
- Equipment and system requirements
- Item-specific carrier characteristics
- Note

Note that illustrative matter is not covered here, but is found in chapter 7 "Describing Content." Illustrative matter is considered to be an attribute of an expression rather than of a manifestation. Similarly, we would need to consult chapter 7 to record color of moving images, presence of sound content, and aspect ratio details (widescreen or full screen).

Section 1: Chapter 4: Acquisitions and Access Information

Those elements considered most useful for helping a user to *obtain* or *access* a resource are covered in chapter 4. They fall under the following general categories:

- Terms of availability

- Contact information

- Restrictions on access

- Restrictions on use

- Uniform resource locator

Information on access is not tied to a preferred source of information and can be taken from any source. Some of this information is used more often in descriptions of archival collections (e.g., restrictions on access and use, contact information). The terms of availability element (rule 4.2.1.2) includes price information, which can be recorded with the ISBN in the MARC 020 field. A uniform resource locator can be included to provide online access to a remote resource.

Chapter 4 is the last chapter in part 1, whose four chapters cover much of what we normally see in the descriptive portion of a bibliographic record.

Section 2: Attributes of Work and Expression

Section 2 of RDA leaves manifestations and items and turns its attention to recording information about works and expressions. Its three chapters are:

- General Guidelines on Recording Attributes of Works and Expressions

- Identifying Works and Expressions

- Describing Content

Section 2: Chapter 5: General Guidelines

Chapter 5 provides definitions and guidelines on describing works and expressions. It defines terms, reviews objectives and principles, and identifies the core elements. RDA uses FRBR's definitions for work and expression. A work is "a distinct intellectual or artistic creation," and an expression is "the intellectual or artistic realization of a work in the form of alpha-numeric, musical or choreographic notation, sound, image, object, movement, etc., or any combination of such forms" (RDA 5.1.2). The objectives for recording attributes of works and expressions are related to the user tasks to find, identify, and select a work.

Section 2: Chapter 6: Identifying Works and Expressions

Chapter 6 is quite lengthy and much of it deals with guidelines on choosing, recording, and constructing preferred and variant titles for works, and as such, is out of scope of the current discussion.

Chapter 6 does, however, include instructions for recording content type (RDA 6.10). Content type is a core element for expressions to be recorded in the bibliographic record in the new MARC field 336. Content types are meant to designate broad categories. Examples of the content types listed in RDA are computer dataset or program, notated or performed music, notated movement, spoken word, still image, and two- or three-dimensional moving image.

Chapter 6 also includes instructions for the elements Form of Work (6.3.1), Other Distinguishing Characteristic of the Work (6.6), and Other Distinguishing Characteristics of the Expression (6.13). These three elements may be included in bibliographic or authority records when coded in MARC 21.

Section 2: Chapter 7: Describing Content

Chapter 7 is the last chapter in section 2 and covers describing content for works and expressions. Some of the elements that will be familiar will be:

- Intended audience
- Summarization of the content
- Place and date of capture (place/date associated with date of recording, filming, etc., of a resource)
- Language of the content
- Illustrative content

- Supplementary content

- Color content

- Sound content

- Aspect ratio (used with moving images, e.g., widescreen DVD)

- Duration

- Performer, narrator, and/or presenter

- Artistic and/or technical credits

- Awards

Note that not all elements will pertain to a given resource and only those appropriate should be included in a bibliographic description. For instance, a book would not have an aspect ratio and you would not include this in its description.

In the MARC 21 environment, these elements may be recorded in coded fields (e.g., the 033 coded field for place and date of capture), in the physical description (3XX) field (e.g., the presence of illustrations) or in notes (5XX) fields (e.g., a summary note or intended audience).

Sections 3 and 4

Sections 3 and 4 of the Attributes part of RDA turn their attention to FRBR's group 2 and Three Entities (creators and subjects). Section 3, "Recording Attributes of Person, Family, and Corporate Body," contains chapters 8–11 and covers guidelines for recording attributes of the group 2 entities. Section 4, "Recording Attributes of Concept, Object, Event, and Place" contains placeholders for chapters 12–15, and chapter 16, "Identifying Places." Chapters 12–15 will cover the subject entities—concepts, objects, and events—but these chapters are not part of RDA's initial launch. The missing chapters will be filled out as work on FRSAD develops. Chapter 16, "Identifying Places," is included in RDA now and covers rules for recording the attributes of Places.

Using the *RDA Toolkit*

In this chapter we looked a bit at what cataloging might be like using RDA. We concentrated on the descriptive parts of cataloging as a way to get our feet wet in the new cataloging code. In doing so, we dealt mostly with sections 1 and 2 (chapters 1–7). Using RDA in conjunction with the MARC 21 format will initially be something of a hunt and peck kind of game. There will be a lot of figuring out where in RDA a familiar AACR2 rule appears. Once found, the rule will need to be reviewed to see if it is the same as AACR2 or has changed. There will also be some amount of matching RDA elements to existing and new fields and subfields of the MARC 21 format, since the correlation is not always clear. Appendix D, "Record Syntaxes for Descriptive Data," provides a helpful guide for this task.

The online product, *RDA Toolkit,* should also make some of this easier. The *Toolkit* offers multiple approaches to navigating RDA content. There are three main tabs (sections) in the *Toolkit*—RDA, Tools, and Resources. You'll find RDA content under the RDA tab. You can browse through the rules using the table of contents tree structure to move to particular sections. There's also a search interface where you can enter a search term and limit in various ways (for example, limit to core elements only or search rules dealing with a specific media type). You can also search by AACR2 rule number. Enter an AACR2 rule, and the search returns a list of RDA rules that deal with the same issue. In the Tools tab, you'll find ways to link between RDA rules and MARC 21 fields. A section on mappings includes a chart showing those RDA fields that are recorded in what MARC fields. In another area of Tools, links will take you into the Library of Congress MARC 21 documentation. Workflows are also found under the Tools tab. This is an area where you can create your own customized documents pertaining to how you need to use RDA. As an example, the section contains a "Simple Book" workflow that walks through the steps for cataloging a book. To create a workflow, you can cut and paste using a word processing-like interface. You can save a workflow in the *Toolkit* or as a PDF file for external use. Finally, the Resource tab contains the full text of AACR2 with links back into RDA (Linker). Hence, the online *Toolkit* anticipates some of the difficulties of learning to use RDA and provides tools for streamlining the process.

CHAPTER 9

RDA and Library Systems

Library system vendors also have a role in RDA implementation. Even with RDA finished and available online, and with many needed MARC changes defined and approved, most libraries need to see changes in their integrated library systems (ILS) before they can implement RDA.

The good news is that, in the short term, library systems won't need to change that much to implement RDA. Because of the need to maintain compatibility with our legacy MARC data, library systems have more tweaking than fundamental changes to make. However, some changes are necessary. In addition, system vendors may want to leverage the opportunities offered in RDA to enhance their existing cataloging modules or public catalog capabilities.

System vendors anxiously awaited the official release of RDA's online product (June 2010) as well as the MARC changes to fields and codes (MARC Updates 10 and 11, October 2009 and February 2010). These components needed to be ready before changes could be made to library systems. In addition, the decision by the national libraries in the United States (Library of Congress, National Library of Medicine, and the National Agricultural Library) to organize a test period before deciding whether to implement RDA made the implementation timetable for U.S. libraries unclear. Many libraries may wait for this decision before moving forward on their own. In spite of delays, some changes are necessary and others warrant consideration.

MARC Changes

A variety of changes in the MARC 21 format were approved to accommodate RDA changes for the bibliographic, holdings, and authority formats.

- New fields were defined for content type (336), media type (337), and carrier type (338).

- New codes in bibliographic fields 007 and 008 were defined.

- In the authority format, fields were added for some of the new RDA elements pertaining to persons, families, and corporate bodies.

- Fields and subfields have been defined or adjusted to accommodate relationship identifiers from RDA appendices I, J, and K in both authority and bibliographic formats.

System vendors need to ensure that their systems accommodate these new fields, codes, and changes.

Indexing Issues

New MARC fields necessitate looking at indexing and indexes in library systems as well. Decisions on whether, and if so, how, to index these fields need to be made at both the vendor and individual library level. System vendors have to make indexing these fields possible and libraries may have further local decisions to make about what they want for their particular situation.

Retrospective Changes

Because RDA set a goal of backward compatibility with existing AACR2 data, there are not too many situations where large groups of records will need retrospective changes. One correction that will need to be looked at is the treatment of Bible headings in RDA. In AACR2, Old Testament is abbreviated "O.T." and New Testament is abbreviated "N.T." In RDA, their titles are spelled out. Further, where AACR2 calls for "N.T." or "O.T." to be interposed between "Bible" and particular books of the Bible, RDA does not. These changes will result in new forms of headings. Hence, libraries will need to deal with existing records with the old forms of headings.

Libraries may also look at existing GMDs in their records. If new cataloging using RDA does not include GMDs, libraries may not want existing GMDs to remain in records. While removing GMDs might be possible in batch jobs, adding the correct content, carrier, and media types could be problematic. Correcting these situations may be something system vendors will institute or they may be projects done at the library level, but both are big enough to warrant examination.

Public Catalog Possibilities: Content, Carrier, and Media Type

In addition to adding the new MARC fields for content, carrier, and media types in their ILS, vendors (and libraries) need to make decisions on how to use the new fields in the public catalog. At a minimum, display of the information in the new fields must be possible. Ensuring that the displayed information is clear and useful to catalog users is a further important step.

Integration of RDA Online into Cataloging Modules

Making RDA available as an online product opens opportunities for its integration with library systems. The publishers of *RDA Toolkit* have expressed a desire to work with other groups on these kinds of initiatives. Vendors might offer context-sensitive help by linking to RDA online from within their cataloging modules.

The changes discussed here can be made in the short term to accommodate and enhance RDA's implementation. The longer term holds more questions, challenges, and excitement.

Database Changes and FRBR-ization

While it is possible to implement RDA using current database structures, many believe we would do better to use structures that more closely reflect the FRBR and FRAD conceptual model. Most library systems rely on bibliographic and authority records to describe resources, access points, and relationships. If we move to a full FRBR/FRAD environment, we may devise new kinds of records or possibly completely different structures. We might have work, expression, manifestation, and item records, with links between these records and related name and subject records. There is even talk of a record-less scenario, where separate elements stand on their own and are brought together on an as-needed basis through linking.

Most now agree that some kind of FRBR-ized display of search results is desirable in our public catalogs. Whether we get there by truly FRBR-izing our entire cataloging process (and data structure) or by manipulating displays at the output stage remains to be seen. In either case, the end goal is an intuitive, user-friendly interface that encourages and enhances discovery by our catalog users.

Post-MARC

And what about MARC? Has it served its purpose? Do we need to move to other data formats for representing and exchanging our bibliographic data? The Library of Congress has already developed MARCXML, which allows MARC data to be shared in the Web environment. If getting our bibliographic data out on the Web is a goal of RDA, then moving to MARCXML or something else might be an option toward getting there.

Semantic Web

Which brings us to the Semantic Web and our next chapter. When RDA developers partnered with the Dublin Core Metadata Initiative, they sought to explore how RDA could move cataloging data out of our library silos and onto the Semantic Web. If our data is Web-bound, should our working platform also become the Web?

Conclusion

Essentially, there are two aspects of RDA implementation to be considered for our library systems. In the short term, there are questions about indexing for the new MARC fields, issues of retrospectively changing existing data to match what RDA now calls for, and possibilities for improving our public catalogs. In the longer term, there are larger issues to be resolved. What is the future for FRBR, FRAD, and FRSAD? Will the library community be able to fully implement these models in cataloging practice? If so, what will it mean for library systems—for cataloging modules and public catalogs? Further, if the library community opts to move away from MARC, how will we migrate our existing MARC records? And finally, if the Semantic Web becomes reality, how will libraries and their integrated library systems adapt?

The Metadata Community

We ended the last chapter with a glimpse into the future, looking at long-term scenarios for library systems. In the next two chapters, we continue to peer into RDA's future, but from the perspective of things happening now in the metadata and Semantic Web community. This chapter introduces the DCMI/RDA Task Group and looks at the tools it uses to ensure that RDA is Web-friendly.

How We Got Here: The DCMI/RDA Task Group

In 2005, following community review of the AACR3 draft, the JSC changed the rules' name to Resource Description and Access (RDA), decided to tie RDA's content and structure more closely to FRBR and FRAD models, and acknowledged the need to work with the metadata community in future RDA development ("Outcomes" 2005).

Toward that end, in April 2007, the Dublin Core Metadata Initiative (DCMI) and others from the metadata community met with members of the JSC at the British Library for a Data Model Meeting ("Data Model Meeting"). The purpose of the meeting was to compare RDA to other metadata data models. As a result of the meeting, DCMI and the RDA Committee of Principals agreed to work together to seek funding for the following goals:

- Development of an RDA element vocabulary

- Development of an RDA Dublin Core application profile based on FRBR and FRAD

- Disclosure of RDA value vocabularies

By April 2008, funding had been secured and the work of the DCMI/ RDA Task Group had begun. Their goals and work plans are recorded on the DCMI/RDA Task Group Wiki, http://dublincore.org/dcmir dataskgroup/ ("DCMI/RDA"). Their output can be found at the National Science Digital Library Metadata Registry, http://metadataregistry. org/ ("NSDL Registry").

What Is the Dublin Core Metadata Initiative?

The Dublin Core Metadata Initiative (DCMI) is a not-for-profit international organization that seeks to encourage and develop standards for the interoperability of metadata ("Dublin Core"). It has strong connections to the library field through OCLC's participation in its founding and development. The Dublin Core element set gets its name from OCLC's home base in Dublin, Ohio. Today it is a much broader coalition of organizations, all interested in sharing metadata on the Web.

What Is the NSDL Registry?

The NSDL Registry supports development of the Semantic Web by providing a place for communities to register their metadata schemes, schemas, and application profiles ("About the Registry"). It uses the building blocks of the Semantic Web to do so; namely, the Resource Description Framework (RDF) and RDF schema (rdfs).

What Is the Semantic Web?

The Semantic Web is an extension of the World Wide Web, a "Giant Global Graph" as Tim Berners-Lee has called it (Berners-Lee). Berners-Lee is credited with inventing the World Wide Web and coining the phrase Semantic Web. Rather like locating documents using URLs, the Semantic Web seeks to identify data using URIs—uniform resource identifiers (Herman 1.1). It seeks to define a structure for data such that computers are able to express and analyze relationships between them ("Semantic Web"). It takes the principles of the Web and applies them to data, with the end result a Semantic Web acting as a vast database.

What Is RDF?

The Resource Description Framework (RDF) offers a means to construct the Semantic Web. It is a "standard model for data interchange on the Web" (Herman 4.1). It provides a structured way to describe resources such that they can be shared and used across applications. RDF breaks information about resources down into single statements. Each statement describes a single characteristic about a resource. RDF statements are comprised of three parts and are called triples. The pieces of a triple are its subject, predicate, and object (MSDN).

- The **subject** is the *resource* that the statement is describing.

- The **predicate** specifies a particular category of characteristic that can be used to describe the resource and is frequently referred to as a *property*.

- The **object** is the *value* of the predicate. The object in a triple can be a "literal," a concrete data value such as a text string or integer or it can be another subject or resource.

For example, Irving Berlin wrote the music and lyrics to the song "Cheek to Cheek." We can construct a triple to express this:

Subject/Resource: The song "Cheek to Cheek"
Predicate/Property: Composer
Object/Value: Irving Berlin

RDF triples are often illustrated as an RDF graph. In the graph model, the subject and object are nodes, connected by an arc, the predicate (Klyne and Carroll). Our Irving Berlin example could be depicted as:

Figure 12: RDF Graph

To ensure that RDF statements uniquely identify the concepts and components used in a given triple, RDF uses Uniform Resource Identifiers (URIs).

Uniform Resource Identifier References

A URI is a unique identifier for an object or resource. Two types of URI are a URL (Uniform Resource Locator) or a URN (Uniform Resource Name). URIs can identify things on the Web, but can also identify things not on the Web. ISBNs are used as URNs because they can uniquely identify a published resource, regardless of whether the resource itself is available on the Web. A URI can be used to identify anything, including persons, companies, and even concepts. RDF uses URI references to designate subjects, predicates, and objects. (Manola and Miller 2.1). URI references point to registered vocabularies where the terms identified by the URIs are defined. For example, the term "composer" is defined in the RDA Roles Element Set at the National Science Digital Library's Registry (http://metadataregistry.org/schema/show/id/4.html). Different groups can register vocabularies and designate URIs for the concepts (subjects, predicates, and objects) that pertain to their community of interest.

Using URI references, the song example might be expressed:

Subject/Resource: http://examplemusic.org/songID/4567

Predicate/Property: http://RDVocab.info/roles/composer

Object/Value: examplemusic.org/personID/32

(Note: http://examplemusic.org does not exist and is made up for our example.)

XML Namespace and Qname

A namespace is simply the place (or space) on the Web where a complete cited URI reference is defined. Namespace is often described as a container or folder that holds a set of related terms. The first part of a URI reference specifies the namespace, which will be the same for all terms to be contained in that namespace (folder). The last part of the URI reference is the local name or specific term used. Using the complete URI can make RDF statements quite long. To shorten them, RDF uses an XML convention called the XML qualified name (Qname).

The Qname can be used to stand in for the namespace portion of a URI reference (Manola and Miller 2.2).

The Dublin Core Element Set (http://dublincore.org/documents/dces/) can be used to illustrate the concepts of namespace and Qnames.

- The namespace for Dublin Core elements is: http://purl.org/dc/elements/1.1/. It is the prefix for each of the specific terms in the set.
- The Dublin Core element "Creator" has the URI reference http://purl.org/dc/elements/1.1/creator
- The Dublin Core element "Date" has the URI reference http://purl.org/dc/elements/1.1/date
- The Dublin Core XML Qname is "dc"
- In RDF, the "Creator" and "Date" elements can be shortened to dc:creator and dc:date

---

RDF/XML

While URIs enable precise identification of resources, RDF statements still need to be encoded (or serialized) in order to be machine-processable. To accomplish this, RDF uses the Extensible Markup Language (XML), specifically RDF/XML, a syntax developed specifically for this purpose (Palmer). Expressing RDF in RDF/XML enables it to be processed and interpreted by other tools and applications on the Web.

RDF Vocabularies and the RDF Schema

An RDF vocabulary defines terms specific to a certain sphere of activity or interest. User communities establish vocabularies, which can be any group that has decided to use RDF as a way to share their specific data on the Web. Each term in an RDF vocabulary resides in a shared namespace and, within it, is assigned a unique URI. For example, the Dublin Core Metadata Initiative established and maintains an RDF vocabulary for the Dublin Core Element Set.

The RDF schema, an extension of RDF, is used to construct RDF vocabularies. Also called the *RDF vocabulary description language,* the RDF schema uses a class and property system (a type system) for describing the properties of resources by domain and range.

Conclusion

In this chapter, we introduced the DCMI/RDA Task Group and reviewed RDF, RDF Schema, namespaces, URIs, and XML as tools for building the Semantic Web. Now it's time to look at how RDA and the Semantic Web can be brought together.

CHAPTER 11

RDA and Metadata

In this chapter, we look at how the DCMI/RDA Task Group uses RDF tools to fulfill their charge and then look at similar activities at the Library of Congress. Both initiatives have important roles to play in bringing cataloging data to the Web.

DCMI/RDA Task Group

The DCMI/RDA Task Group had the following goals:

- Develop an RDA element vocabulary
- Develop an RDA Dublin Core application profile based on FRBR and FRAD
- Register the RDA value vocabularies

The group's charter was to "define components of the draft standard *RDA—Resource Description and Access* as an RDF vocabulary for use in developing a Dublin Core application profile" ("DCMI/RDA").

Development of an RDA Element Vocabulary

To develop the RDA element vocabulary, the group used the entity relationship diagrams created as part of RDA online (Hillmann, Coyle, Phipps, and Dunsire). The diagrams are available on the *RDA Toolkit*

Web site at http://www.rdatoolkit.org/background. The elements delineated in these diagrams were used for building the RDA Element Sets at the NSDL *Registry*. Note that both RDA elements (FRBR attributes) and FRBR relationships are defined as RDF properties in the following element sets. The FRBR entities (WEMI, etc.) are defined as classes (Coyle, "RDA" 27).

- FRBR Entities for RDA
    - The FRBR entities are defined as RDF classes in this element set.
- RDA Group 1 Elements
    - This element set lists the elements in RDA that pertain to works, expressions, manifestations, or items (the attributes of the group 1 entities from FRBR).
- RDA Group 2 Elements
    - This set of properties and subproperties corresponds to elements describing persons, families, or corporate bodies, the group 2 entities in FRBR.
- RDA Group 3 Elements
    - The group 3 elements are those elements of RDA that describe concepts, objects, events, and places.
- RDA Relationships for Works, Expressions, Manifestations, Items
    - The relationships listed in appendix J of RDA are defined as properties and subproperties in this element set.
- RDA Relationships for Persons, Corporate Bodies, Families
    - The relationships between persons, families, and corporate bodies that are listed in appendix K of RDA are defined here.
- RDA Relationships for Concepts, Events, Objects, Places
    - The basic relationships between concepts, events, objects, and places are defined here. Appendix L of RDA will contain the specific relationship terms when they are defined.
- RDA Roles
    - This element set correlates to appendix I of RDA "Relationship Designators: Relationships between a Resource and Persons, Families, and Corporate Bodies Associated with the Resource."

You can see these element lists at the NSDL Registry (http://meta dataregistry.org/rdabrowse.htm).

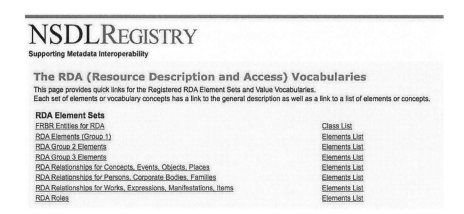

Figure 13: RDA Element Sets at the NSDL Registry

Source: NSDL Registry (National Science Digital Library). Used with permission.

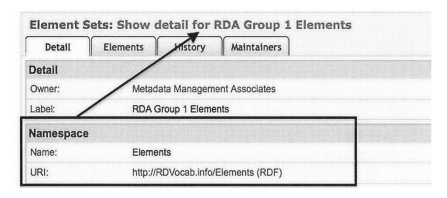

Figure 14: Namespace for RDA Group 1 Elements

Source: NSDL Registry (National Science Digital Library). Used with permission.

Each element set has a namespace, and each element has been assigned its own URI.

An RDA Dublin Core Application Profile Based on FRBR/FRAD

A second goal in developing the RDA vocabulary was to develop a Dublin Core (DC) application profile for RDA. Application profiles enable interoperability between metadata while offering flexibility for local practice and implementation (Heery and Patel 1). They also define constraints (rules) for using the data elements in the profile

(Coyle, "RDA" 34). The DCMI/RDA Task Group has developed two RDA application profiles that can be found at http://dublincore.org/dcmirdataskgroup/rda_2da.

Disclosure of RDA Value Vocabularies Using RDF/RDFS/SKOS

The last goal in the RDA vocabularies project was to develop vocabularies for the many lists of values provided within RDA. These are described as "in-line vocabularies" because they appear within the text of RDA. There are more than 50 of these lists or vocabularies in RDA ("RDAVocab"). An example is the list of media types supplied in chapter 3 of RDA at section 3.2.1.2 (table 3.1). Catalogers are instructed to assign one of the listed media types—audio, computer, microform, microscopic, projected, stereographic, unmediated, video—to the resource being described. Taking these lists from within RDA and publishing them as controlled vocabularies at the NSDL Registry was the third goal agreed at the British Library meeting in 2005.

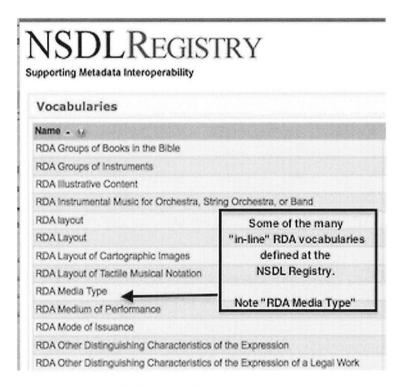

Figure 15: RDA In-Line Vocabularies on the NSDL Registry

Source: NSDL Registry (National Science Digital Library). Used with permission.

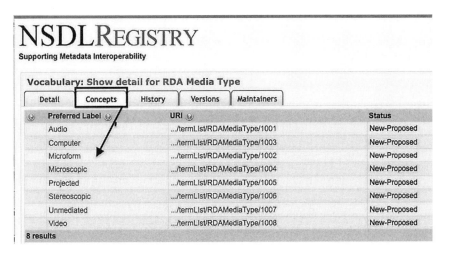

Figure 16: RDA Media Type Concepts

Source: NSDL Registry (National Science Digital Library). Used with permission.

The DCMI/RDA Task Force chose SKOS, the Simple Knowledge Organization System, to produce these lists. SKOS is an application of RDF, designed specifically for controlled vocabularies and other concept schemes (Isaac and Summers). These in-line vocabularies are located in the vocabularies section of the NSDL Registry (http://meta dataregistry.org/vocabulary/list.html).

The concepts listed for the RDA media type vocabulary match the terms that appear in RDA's in-line list given in table 3.1 at section 3.2.

Library of Congress Authorities and Vocabularies Service

In Spring 2009, the Library of Congress announced the launch of its authorities and vocabularies service (Redding). Its goal is to offer LC's many vocabularies and thesauri as vocabularies with URIs so that machines may manipulate the data. The LC subject headings were the first offering. They are currently available for browse searching or for download as RDF/XML or N-Triples formats at the Library of Congress Web site ("Library of Congress Authorities" http://id.loc.gov/authorities/). There are over 350,000 subject headings included in the service. LC plans to make other vocabularies available, such as the code lists for MARC Relator, Language, Country, and Geographic Area. Like the RDA Vocabularies, this service provides URIs that can be used to uniquely identify a term and can be used as part of an RDF triple.

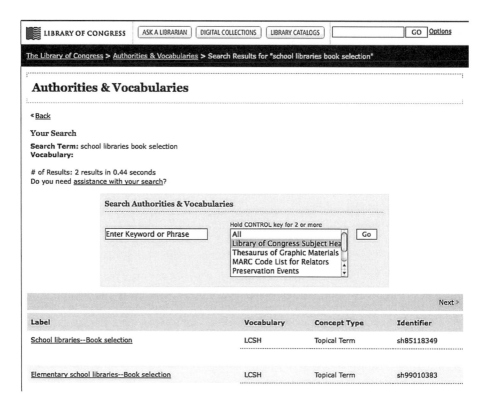

Figure 17: Library of Congress Authorities and Vocabularies Service

Source: Library of Congress. Used with permission.

Figure 18: LC Authorities and Vocabularies: URI

Source: Library of Congress. Used with permission.

A New Catalog Record?

What are catalogers and libraries supposed to do with all this? Well, that remains to be seen to some extent. In some scenarios, librarians imagine entering links (URIs) into bibliographic records. Assuming that language codes, relator codes, and other vocabularies join LC's subject headings and RDA's value vocabularies in having assigned URIs, this becomes possible. Others go further and suggest that we need either new kinds of record formats or perhaps a completely new approach with no records at all.

Which, if any, of these scenarios will come to pass is still uncertain. What is certain is that the DCMI/RDA Task Group and LC are working to open the window of opportunity for the library community and library data. Without this work, RDA would hold much less potential for meeting the need or demand for Web-accessible data in the long term. With this work, anyone in the metadata community can make use of either or both RDA elements and LC subject headings. Closer to home, inside libraries, these projects make it possible for traditional cataloging processes to morph into metadata production, with the end goal being cataloging data that lives and thrives and gets used on the Semantic Web.

CHAPTER 12

RDA and You

RDA will impact all libraries, but perhaps on different timelines and in varying ways. For all libraries, there will be an initial MARC-based implementation phase followed by a second phase where MARC may be replaced and our data may move to the Semantic Web. This final chapter looks at the decisions to be made for implementing RDA in the short term and at the changes your library can expect as a result. In addition, we'll look at the long-term implications and possibilities.

Planning

When developing an implementation plan for RDA in your library, you'll need to consider:

- Timeline
- Budget
- Training

The trickiest piece may be the timeline because it will perforce depend on forces outside your control. The following pieces need to be in place before you can determine an implementation target date:

- Your library system vendor must provide upgraded software to accommodate MARC changes.
- The suppliers of your MARC records (e.g., a bibliographic utility such as OCLC or your book vendors, for example, Baker & Taylor)

need to implement RDA to be able to provide RDA-based cataloging records.

Many libraries, possibly yours, may wish to defer decisions on RDA until after the testing period by the U.S. National Libraries. The National Libraries have set up a Web site where the testing process can be followed: http://www.loc.gov/bibliographic-future/rda/ ("Testing RDA"). Training and testing are scheduled for July through December 2010. Evaluation will take an additional three months, at which point a report of findings will be shared with the library community. Many in the library community expect that general adoption of RDA will not begin until June 2011 and later for many libraries.

As for system upgrades, vendors may be ready with software changes before or around the time that U.S. testing of RDA concludes. Once your vendor has an upgrade ready, you will want to schedule it at a time that makes sense for your library.

Budgeting and purchasing decisions for RDA must also be made in your library. Should your library subscribe to the online *RDA Toolkit* or will purchasing the print version of RDA meet your cataloging needs? As a subscription product, *RDA Toolkit* represents an ongoing budget item while the print edition is a once-off cost. Basic pricing for the *Toolkit* was announced at ALA Midwinter in January 2010 and is available at the RDA Web site (http://www.rdatoolkit.org/).

Training will be another component of budgeting for RDA. Formal training programs will be developed as the toolkit is available and feedback on the testing process becomes available.

Because RDA is designed to be backward compatible, there are not an excessive number of new rules to learn. However, training should cover the changes that *were* made, including no more Rule of Three, fewer abbreviations, changes to transcription policy, and content, carrier, and media type changes. For those used to using AACR2 in print, a major challenge in training may be getting used to the online product. For newer catalogers, the online environment may be familiar, but RDA's rules and structure may present the larger learning curve. In addition, for some, training will need to include review of FRBR and FRAD concepts so that RDA can make sense.

Implementation

Once you have upgraded your library system, confirmed that your bibliographic utility and materials vendors are RDA-compliant, and subscribed to the *RDA Toolkit*, you'll want to evaluate how and where RDA has affected existing data as well as the public catalog.

With regard to existing catalog records, you might decide that some RDA changes are big enough that your existing data should be changed to agree with it. Two possibilities are making retrospective changes to Bible headings in your existing records and what to do about defunct General Material Designators (GMDs). It's possible that your vendor may assist with the decisions or the process here. Your library may also want to look at how RDA's MARC changes have impacted previous indexing decisions for your database. At the least, you want to know how new MARC fields have been indexed. You may also want to make additional indexing changes.

It's equally, if not more, important to see how RDA implementation has affected your public catalog. Make sure to see what has happened with GMDs and with the new MARC fields for content, carrier, and media types. Are there helpful displays for your users? If not, can you make changes to improve the situation? Do changes in user displays necessitate or suggest additional retrospective changes to your existing data?

Once you have decided what kind of retrospective cleanups and other changes you want to make, you are ready to start cataloging using the initial implementation of RDA and MARC 21 for encoding.

The Future

It's important to remember that the upcoming implementation of RDA is just the beginning. There are still questions about what will happen next. Many are hoping that our library data will make the leap onto the Semantic Web. If the MARC format is left behind, and a new container such as MARCXML or some other option is adapted, then cataloging data will be more accessible than in the MARC environment. It will be easier to extract it from wherever it lives and easier to repurpose it. Given that many librarians in all areas of library work are now familiar with a variety of Web tools, data created for the Web will be more accessible to them than a record in MARC. For this, and other reasons, removing this constraint on our data might be the best thing that comes out of RDA.

Works Cited

"AACR (Anglo-American Cataloging Rules) Governance." *Anglo-American Cataloguing Rules.* American Library Association, Canadian Library Association, Chartered Institute of Library and Information Professionals, c2006. Web. 3/5/2010 http://www.aacr2.org/governance.html.

AACR2: Anglo-American Cataloguing Rules, Second Edition, 2002 Revision, 2005 Update. Chicago: American Library Association, c2005. Print.

"About the Registry." *NSDL Registry.* National Science Digital Library. n.d. Web. 3/5/2010 http://metadataregistry.org/about.html.

Baden, Diane. *Is FRBR in our future?* ILL Spring meeting. NELINET, Southborough, MA. 16 June 2003. Presentation.

Berners-Lee, Tim. "Giant Global Graph." *DIG blog.* Computer Science and Artificial Intelligence Laboratory. Massachusetts Institute of Technology. 21 November 2007. Web. 3/5/2010 http://dig.csail.mit.edu/breadcrumbs/node/215.

Coyle, Karen. "RDA Vocabularies for a Twenty-First-Century Data Environment." *Library Technology Reports.* February/March 2010. Print.

"Data Model Meeting. British Library, London, 30 April–1 May 2007." *The British Library. Bibliographic Department.* The British Library, n.d. Web. 10/26/2009 http://www.bl.uk/bibliographic/meeting.html.

DCMI/RDA Task Group Wiki. Dublin Core Metadata Initiative, n.d. Web. 3/5/2010 http://dublincore.org/dcmirdataskgroup/FrontPage.

"Draft of AACR3 Part I—Background." *Joint Steering Committee for Development of RDA. Historic Documents.* JSC RDA, n.d. Web. 3/5/2010 http://www.rda-jsc.org/aacr3draftpt1.html.

Dublin Core Metadata Initiative. DCMI, c1995–2009. Web. 10/26/2009 http://dublincore.org/.

FRAD: Functional Requirements for Authority Data: A Conceptual Model (Draft 2007-04-01). IFLA Working Group on Functional Requirements and Numbering of Authority Records (FRANAR), 2007. PDF file.

FRBR: Functional Requirements for Bibliographic Records: Final Report. As amended and corrected through February 2009. International Federation of Library Associations and Institutions, 2009. PDF File. http://www.ifla.org/files/cataloguing/frbr/frbr_2008.pdf.

FRSAD: Functional Requirement for Subject Authority Data: A Conceptual Model. 2nd Draft 2009–06–10. IFLA Working Group on Functional Requirements for Subject Authority Records (FRSAR), 2009. PDF file. http://nkos.slis.kent.edu/FRSAR/report090623.pdf.

Glennan, Kathy. *From AACR2 to RDA: An Evolution.* Music Library Association. Bibliographic Control Committee. 2006. PDF File. www.musiclibraryassoc.org/BCC/Descriptive/RDA_Evolution.pdf.

Heery, Rachel and Manjula Patel. "Application profiles: mixing and matching metadata schemas." *Ariadne.* UKOLN. Issue 25. 24 September 2000. Web. 3/5/2010 http://www.ariadne.ac.uk/issue25/app-profiles/intro.html.

Herman, Ivan (maintained by). "W3C Semantic Web Frequently Asked Questions." *W3C Semantic Web.* W3C. c1994–2009. Web. 3/5/2010 http://www.w3.org/RDF/FAQ.

Hillmann, Diane, Karen Coyle, Jon Phipps, and Gordon Dunsire. "RDA Vocabularies: Process, Outcome Use." *D-Lib Magazine.* Corporation for National Research Initiatives (CNRI), January/February 2010. Web. 03/02/2010 http://www.dlib.org/dlib/january10/hillmann/01hillmann.html.

Isaac, Antoine and Ed Summers, editors. *SKOS Simple Knowledge Organization System Primer: W3C Working Group Note 18 August 2009."* W3C, 2009. Web. 3/5/2010 http://www.w3.org/TR/skos-primer/.

Klyne, Graham and Jeremy J. Carroll, editors. "Graph Data Model, Section 3.1." *Resource Description Framework (RDF): Concepts and Abstract Syntax.* W3C. c2004. Web. 3/5/2010 http://www.w3.org/TR/rdf-concepts/#section-data-model.

Library of Congress Authorities & Vocabularies. Library of Congress, n.d. Web. 3/5/2010 http://id.loc.gov/authorities/.

Library of Congress Working Group on the Future of Bibliographic Control. *On the Record: Report of the Library of Congress Working Group on the Future of Bibliographic Control.* Library of Congress, 2008. PDF File. http://www.loc.gov/bibliographic-future/news/lcwg-ontherecord-jan08-final.pdf.

Linker, Troy. *RDA Toolkit—A Guided Tour—02/09/2010.* Webinar video. 6/5/2010 http://www.rdatoolkit.org/training/guidedtour.

Manola, Frank and Eric Miller, editors. "2.1 Basic Concepts" *RDF Primer.* Version: 10 February 2004. W3C. c2004. Web. 3/5/2010 http://www.w3.org/TR/rdf-primer/#basicconcepts.

Manola, Frank and Eric Miller, editors. "2.2 The RDF Model." *RDF Primer.* Version: 10 February 2004. W3C. c2004. Web. 3/5/2010 http://www.w3.org/TR/rdf-primer/#rdfmodel.

"MARC 21 Format 2009 Changes to Accommodate RDA (Draft)." *MARC Standards.* The Library of Congress, July 17, 2009. Web. 3/5/2010 http://www.loc.gov/marc/formatchanges-RDA.html.

Marcum, Deanna B. *Response to On the Record: Report of the Library of Congress Working Group on the Future of Bibliographic Control.* Library of Congress, 2008. PDF File. http://www.loc.gov/bibliographic-future/news/LCWGResponse-Marcum-Final-061008.pdf.

Mauer, Margaret Beecher. "Before you attend the workshop: FRBR and the future." *TechKNOW.* Technical Services Division of the Ohio Library

Council. Vol.10, no. 1, March 2004. PDF file. http://www.olc.org/pdf/
TechKNOWMarch2004.pdf.

Maxwell, Robert. FRBR: *A Guide for the Perplexed.* Chicago. American Library
Association. 2008. Print.

MSDN. "What is the Resource Description Framework?" *Microsoft Developer
Network: msdn.* Microsoft Corporation. c2006, 2009. Web. 3/5/2010
http://msdn.microsoft.com/en-us/library/aa303722.aspx.

NSDL Registry. National Science Digital Library, n.d. Web. 3/5/2010 http://
metadataregistry.org/.

"Outcomes of the Meeting of the Joint Steering Committee Held in Chicago,
Illinois, 24–28 April 2005." *Joint Steering Committee for Development
of RDA. Historic Documents.* JSC RDA, 2005. Web. 3/5/2010 http://
www.rda-jsc.org/0504out.html.

"Outcomes of the Meeting of the Joint Steering Committee Held in Chicago, Illinois, 15–20 October 2007." *Joint Steering Committee for Development
of RDA. Historic Documents.* JSC RDA, 2007. Web. 3/5/2010 http://
www.rda-jsc.org/0710out.html.

Palmer, Sean B. "What is the Semantic Web?" *The Semantic Web: An Introduction.* Infomesh.net. 2001. Web. 11/14/2009 http://infomesh.net/2001/
swintro/#whatIsSw.

Patton, Glenn E. "From FRBR to FRAD: Extending the Model." *World Library
and Information Congress: 75th IFLA General Conference and Council.*
Milan, Italy. 23–27 August 2009. PDF file. http://www.ifla.org/files/hq/
papers/ifla75/215-patton-en.pdf.

Powell, Andy, Mikael Nilsson, Ambjörn, Pete Johnston, and Thomas Baker.
DCMI Abstract Model. DCMI, 2007. Web. 3/5/2010 http://dublincore.
org/documents/abstract-model/.

*RDA Brochure: RDA: Resource Description and Access: The Cataloging Stan-
dard for the 21st century.* Joint Steering Committee for Development
of RDA, n.d. PDF file. http://www.rda-jsc.org/docs/rdabrochure-
eng.pdf.

RDA Element Analysis. Joint Steering Committee for Development of RDA,
July 2009. PDF file. http://www.rda-jsc.org/docs/5rda-elementanalysis
rev3.pdf.

"RDA FAQ: Frequently Asked Questions." *Joint Steering Committee for Development of RDA. Historic Documents.* JSC RDA, n.d. Web. 3/5/2010
http://www.rda-jsc.org/rdafaq.html.

RDA Full Draft. American Library Association, Canadian Library Association,
and the Chartered Institute of Library and Information Professionals.
c2006. PDF File. http://www.rdatoolkit.org/constituencyreview/

"RDA in MARC January 2010." *MARC Standards.* The Library of Congress,
29 January 2010. Web. 3/5/2010 http://www.loc.gov/marc/RDAin
MARC29.html.

RDA/ONIX Framework for Resource Categorization. Joint Steering Committee
for the Development of RDA, 2006. PDF file. http://www.rda-jsc.org/
working2.html#chair-10 http://www.loc.gov/marc/marbi/2007/5
chair10.pdf.

"RDA Toolkit." *RDA: Resource Description & Access.* American Library Association, Canadian Library Association, and the Chartered Institute
of Library and Information Professionals. c2010. Web. 6/5/2010 http://
www.rdatoolkit.org/

"RDAVocab. List of RDA Value Vocabularies." DCMI/RDA Task Group Wiki.
Dublin Core Metadata Initiative, n.d. Web. 3/5/2010 http://dublincore.
org/dcmirdataskgroup/RDAVocab.

Redding, Clay. *Library of Congress Controlled Vocabularies as Linked Data:
http:id.loc.gov.* Digital Library Federation Spring Forum. Raleigh,
North Carolina, 2009. PDF file. http://www.diglib.org/forums/
spring2009/presentations/Redding.pdf.

Rust, Godfrey and Mark Bide. "The <indecs> metadata framework: Principles,
model and data dictionary." June 2000. PDF file. www.doi.org/topics/
indecs/indecs_framework_2000.pdf.

Schwartz, Christine. "RDA/MARC working group established." *Cataloging
Futures.* 14 March 2008. Web. 3/5/2010 http://www.catalogingfutures.
com/catalogingfutures/2008/03/rdamarc-working.html.

"Semantic Web Tutorial." *w3schools.com.* w3Schools. c1999–2009. Web.
3/5/2010 http://www.w3schools.com/semweb/default.asp.

"Testing Resource Description and Access (RDA)." *Library of Congress. Bibliographic Control Working Group.* Library of Congress. n.d. Web.
3/5/2010 http://www.loc.gov/bibliographic-future/rda/.

Tillett, Barbara. *What is FRBR? A conceptual model for the bibliographic universe.* Library of Congress. Cataloging Distribution Service. rev. February
2004. PDF File. http://www.loc.gov/cds/downloads/FRBR.PDF.

Tillett, Barbara and Ana Lupe Cristán, editors. *IFLA Cataloguing Principles:
Statement of International Cataloguing Principles (ICP) and its Glossary.*
Munich. K.G. Saur, 2009. Print.

Index

entities, 13–18; relationships, 21–24

Functional Requirements for Subject Authority Data (FRSAD), 9

G

General Material Designator, 40–41, 81

GMD. *See* General Material Designator

GMD/SMD Working Group, 41

Group 1 entities, 13–16

Group 2 entities, 16–17

Group 3 entities, 17–18

H

Hierarchical description, 54

I

Identifier (entity), 19–20, 25

IFLA. *See* International Federation of Library Associations and Institutions

IFLA's Meeting of Experts on an International Cataloging Code (IME ICC), 5, 35

Illustrative matter, 56

IME ICC. *See* IFLA's Meeting of Experts on an International Cataloging Code

Integrating resource, 54

International Federation of Library Associations and Institutions (IFLA), 5, 9

International Standard Bibliographic Description (General) (ISBD (G)), 30, 31, 37

ISBD (G). *See* International Standard Bibliographic Description (General)

Item (entity), 15

J

Joint Steering Committee for Revision of AACR (JSC), 2–6, 28, 41, 43, 65

JSC. *See* Joint Steering Committee for Revision of AACR

K

"Known by" relationships, 27

L

Library of Congress Authorities and Vocabularies Service, 75–76

Library of Congress Working Group on the Future on Bibliographic Control, 6

Logical relationships, 21–23

M

Main entry, 30

Manifestation (entity), 15

MARC and RDA, 5, 12, 28; changes in, 45–51; future, 64; library systems and, 62; mapping, 57, 58, 59; *RDA Toolkit* and, 60

Media type (element), 41, 46, 56

Mode of issuance, 54

N

Name (entity), 19

Name authority, 30

Namespace, 68–69, 73

National Science Digital Library Metadata Registry (NSDL), 66, 72–75

NSDL Registry. *See* National Science Digital Library Metadata Registry

O

Object (entity), 17

Object (RDF), 67

"On the Record: Report of the Library of Congress Working Group on the Future of Bibliographic Control," 6

ONIX. *See* ONline Information eXchange

ONline Information eXchange (ONIX), 5, 43

40.00